Bank Capital Structure and Procyclicality of Leverage

Çiydem Çatak

Bank Capital Structure and Procyclicality of Leverage

PETER LANG

Bibliographic Information published by the Deutsche Nationalbibliothek
The Deutsche Nationalbibliothek lists this publication in the Deutsche Nationalbibliografie; detailed bibliographic data is available online at http://dnb.d-nb.de.

Library of Congress Cataloging-in-Publication Data
Names: Catak, Ciydem, 1984- author.
Title: Bank capital structure and procyclicality of leverage / Ciydem Catak.
Description: Berlin ; New York : Peter Lang, [2018]
Identifiers: LCCN 2018014652 | ISBN 9783631746219
Subjects: LCSH: Bank capital--Turkey. | Bank assets--Turkey. | Business cycles--Turkey.
Classification: LCC HG1616.C34 C28 2018 | DDC 332.1--dc23 LC record available at https://lccn.loc.gov/2018014652

ISBN 978-3-631-74621-9 (Print) · E-ISBN 978-3-631-75303-3 (E-PDF)
E-ISBN 978-3-631-75304-0 (EPUB) · E-ISBN 978-3-631-75305-7 (MOBI)
DOI 10.3726/b13845

Peter Lang – Berlin · Bern · Bruxelles · New York · Oxford · Warszawa · Wien

This publication has been peer reviewed.

www.peterlang.com

I would like to thank my supervisor, Prof. Dr. Emin AVCI, for his valuable insights about the topic and The Scientific and Technological Research Council of Turkey (TÜBİTAK) for providing the funding for my Ph.D. degree. I owe particular gratitude to my beloved family, for their endless support and patience.

Çiydem ÇATAK

Table of Contents

List of Tables

List of Figures

Abbreviations

BDDK	Banking Regulation and Supervision Agency
CPI	Consumer Price Index
Euribor- OIS	Euribor Overnight Index Swap
FAS	Financial Accounting Standards
FVA	Fair Value Accounting
GDP	Gross Domestic Product
GMM	Generalized Method of Moments
IFRS	International Financial Reporting Standards
IRB	International Ratings-Based Approach
OECD	Organization for Economic Cooperation and Development
OLS	Ordinary Least Squares
PPP	Purchasing Power Parity
SME	Small and Medium-Sized Enterprises
VaR	Value-at-Risk

1 Introduction

Banks are the most important intermediaries of the financial system and occupy an outstanding position due to their functions within the national economy. Until the 2007 financial crisis, financial market regulations were based on the notion that stability of the financial system can be ensured through measures that provide solvency of each individual bank. However, the importance of systemic risk has been underestimated. In contrast to specific risks, which only affect individual financial market participants, systemic risks affect the functioning of the financial system as a whole. Risks, which are not identifiable or controllable at the bank level, can be mutually reinforced by the aggregation of individual risks and cause a crisis of the system completely. As a result, the micro-prudential level of regulation has been supplemented by the macro-prudential level, which has a basic aim of ensuring the stability of the financial system by limiting systemic risks.

The collapse of the financial system in 2007 also once more brought to light the close link between the financial sector and the real economy. Actually, the financial system was always procyclical. During economic booms, with high asset prices and low interest rates, risks are often underestimated, the value of collateral is surpassed and credit spreads are expanded too far. Low interest rates support innovations that enable banks to further increase their debt levels, thereby increasing their return on equity. As a consequence, leverage increases throughout the system and institutions become increasingly vulnerable even to small price corrections. The necessary reduction of the excessive leverage in the recession additionally strengthens this vulnerability. It should also be noted that this cyclicality of the financial system has been further enhanced in recent years by regulations such as the Basel II accord. The risk weight of assets introduced by Basel II are mapped by means of external or internal ratings, which are typically underestimated in long-term risks in boom phases and must be corrected downwards during downturns. As the banks' capital requirements are smaller in the upturn than in the downturn, there is initially an increased lending expansion, which is followed by a correspondingly larger contraction. Consequently, the amplitude of the overall economic cycle increases.

Another important issue is the leverage effect, which plays an important role in strengthening economic cycles. Capital procurement is difficult to attain during crisis period and banks must either sell asset or increase equity. In most of the cases, banks choose to sell their assets and the prices of the securities are further reduced; such reduction in prices requires additional asset to be sold again until a target or constant leverage ratio is reached. Hence, leverage ratio often behaves procyclically, which means that the leverage ratio increases during periods of boom and conversely, it falls during recessions. With this cyclical behavior of the leverage, economic problems are causing financial problems, and these financial problems are making the already bad economic situation worse. In order to take various measures to eliminate this vicious cycle, we first need to investigate whether there is such a situation in Turkey.

This book attempts to explain the procyclical behavior of Turkish banks leverage and determinants of bank capital structure. The cyclical behavior of leverage began to attract attention with the study of Geanakoplos (2010) and Adrian and Shin (2010). Bank supervisory institutions, which have come to realize the cyclical behavior of leverage ratios of banks, have started to do a lot of work to take measures. Although there are many studies on this subject in a large number of countries, studies on this subject in Turkey are very few. This topic has not been included in the Turkish banking literature, except the work done by Binici and Köksal (2012) and the work done by Çalışkan (2011). Therefore this book contributes to existing literature of leverage behavior by providing empirical analysis from Turkey. The analysis is based on the data of Turkish development and investment, commercial and participation banks for the period of 2005–2014. By using panel data analysis, eight different leverage ratios: the ratio of total assets to total equity, the ratio of total debt to total equity, the ratio of the sum of the total debt and off balance sheet liabilities to total equity, the ratio of the difference between Tier 1 capital and regulatory deductions to the ratio of the sum of the total assets and off balance sheet liabilities, the ratio of the difference between Tier 1 capital and regulatory deductions to the ratio of the sum of the total debt and off balance sheet liabilities, the ratio of Tier 1 capital to adjusted assets and one minus the ratio of total equity to total assets are evaluated. The economic situation is measured by asset growth and it is assumed that if there is a growth in bank assets, there is an economic boom and if there is a decline in bank assets, there is economic recession.

After analyzing the behavior of Turkish banks leverage, the determinants of leverage are also examined. This topic has been studied around the world many times, and there is a lot of explanatory work in the literature. The factors determining the capital structure of banks in Turkey have also been investigated several times. However, the explanatory variables that are similar to each other are used in the studies carried out in general. So, in this study different explanatory variables were added to the model to be different from the other works. Four bank-specific and four macroeconomic variables, eight variables in total used as explanatory variables. Size, collateral, profit, number of banks are evaluated as the bank-specific determinants and gross domestic product (GDP), consumer price index, money supply and exchange rate are evaluated as the macroeconomic determinants of bank capital structure. In order to prevent the biased estimates of the trending variables, a trend term is included into model.

The first section contains an overview of the study with a brief summary of each section. It is also mentioned the purpose and importance of research and its contribution to the literature on the finance.

The remainder of the book is structured as follows. In the second section of this book, the general connection between the financial system and the real economy is briefly discussed and a theoretical framework is outlined. A detailed definition of procyclicality is made and different views are presented together. Additionally, causes of procyclicality listed in the following subheadings: Deviations from the Efficient Market Hypothesis, Credit Rating Agencies, Economic Policy, Basel II, Fair Value Accounting and Leverage. Particular attention is drawn to leverage, which plays a central role in the explanation of procyclical behavior of banks. After determining the behavior of leverage, in the third section we attempt to find the determinants of leverage. Furthermore, the theories that are associated with capital structure are highlighted and empirical researches on the determinants of firms and banks capital structure are emphasized. This section also establishes an understanding of the relationship among selected important bank-specific and macroeconomic variables and Turkish banks leverage ratio.

Section four initially focuses on the research methodology, research design and findings of study. Data and sample selection, variables and descriptive statistics are displayed and evaluated in that section. The details of eight empirical models are discussed and the results of the analysis are explained in depth. Also, the second part of the fourth section includes descriptive statistics, analysis and results for the determinants of bank leverage, bank-specific and macroeconomic explanatory variables as well. The results were compared with those in the literature.

Finally, a general conclusion is given. Meanwhile, the limitations are provided together with the suggestions for further research.

2 Procyclicality

2.1 Definition of procyclicality

Procyclicality is a natural part of the real and financial sectors of an economy which has been taken into much notice with the 2007–2009 financial crisis. It is well documented by many economists that the behavior of banks is procyclical (Gambera, 2000; Salas and Saurina, 2002) and this behavior threatens macroeconomic and financial stability. It is believed that macroeconomic factors are behind each financial crisis (Salas and Saurina, 2002) as financial institutions change their activities based on changing macroeconomic conditions (Athanasoglou and Daniilidis, 2011).

The term procyclicality is used to describe the interaction between the financial sector and the real economy. As defined in the 2009 annual report of Bank for International Settlement's, a procyclical financial system "*refers to the notion that its dynamics and the dynamics of the real economy reinforce each other, increasing the amplitude of booms and busts and undermining stability of both the financial sector and the real economy*". In other words, when the economy is doing well, there is excessive risk-taking and excessive financial activity. On the other hand, when the economy gets worse, there is not enough willingness to take risks and very little financial activity. This behavior may create a situation in which economic problems cause financial problems, which then causes economic problems again, so the whole process continues to be repeated (Hardouvelis, 2010, p. 2). Due to the cyclical behavior of banking sector, banks work as amplifiers and adversely affect financial stability instead of working as a mitigation mechanism and allocating resources efficiently within the economy and provide a stable financial system. The cyclical behavior is likely to ease their lending standards when there is an economic upturn and make it difficult when the conditions become worse (Athanasoglou and Daniilidis, 2011). In periods of expansion, banks underestimate risk and reduce their capital buffer and make their selection criteria less strict, and this system increases the supply of credit. In the opposite case, during recessions there is a high capital buffer ratio, the selection criteria are very strict and there is a decrease in the supply of credit. Also, this system increases the strength of cyclical fluctuations instead of counterbalancing them (Cesaroni, 2015, pp. 62–83).

Nijathaworn (2009) emphasizes that procyclicality is a problem arising from the interaction between the cycles of economy, finance and risk-taking behavior which strengthen or support each other and move in the same direction with fluctuations in asset prices. From another perspective, the financial accelerator mechanism arises from information asymmetries between borrowers and lenders. Information asymmetries emerge in situations where (1) there is not enough economic activity and collateral values are low; or (2) economic conditions become better than before and collateral values increase. In the first case, there is an overestimated risk and the borrowers can't get funding from banks even for profitable projects, whereas in the second case the risk is underestimated and the firms can guarantee funding very easily even for projects that may not be profitable. Hence, it can be concluded that the financial system is procyclical and amplifies business cycle fluctuations (Borio, et al., 2001).

Craig, et al., (2006 argue that procyclicality is a part of the economic system, but the weaknesses of the financial sector may infuriate it and turn it into a threat to macroeconomic and financial stability. These fundamental sector faults can be listed as insufficient risk management, inadequate governance in supervision and dependence on variable sources of funding. Another issue worth emphasizing refers to the interaction between the banking system and financial liberalization. In their study, Demirgüç-Kunt and Detragiache (1998) tried to find out the effect of financial liberalization on the probability of banking crisis. A study of 53 countries shows that banking crisis is more likely to occur in liberalized financial systems. With liberalized financial systems, foreign banks begin to affect domestic banks and influence the cycle with different response (Craig, et al., 2006 p. 4). While the availability of market liberalization and financial innovation allows for new opportunities, it also causes new problems. The first problem refers to the above-mentioned phenomenon that risk is typically underestimated during booms, with less regard to the potential problems it can cause, and overestimated during busts with hypersensitivity towards risk. The second problem is related to regulatory authorities that can make the cyclical behavior of banks worse with the hypothesis "too much too late". That means the slowly developed regulatory solutions to economic and financial problems have always been a potential danger (Lowe and Stevens, 2004). Covas and Fujita (2010) also look at this from a macroeconomic perspective and argue that bank capital regulation can cause "procyclicality", meaning that bank capital regulations can increase the effects or strength of macroeconomic fluctuations. The cyclical behavior of banks was realized with the first Basel accord which imposed specific standards on banks like holding a constant fraction of equity. In addition, there has been an increased interest in the procyclicality issue with the Basel II accord which included risk-sensitive regulation. There is a negative relationship between each loan and borrower's quality. That means when the economy is not doing good and the overall credit quality develops into a bad situation, capital requirements become tighter and banks decrease their lending capacity.

Procyclicality is also clarified as a result of the adoption of risk-sensitive bank capital requirements which affect bank lending volume and exacerbate the change in business cycle. It may be due to systematic risk that arises from macroeconomic factors or from the interdependencies of financial markets and international institutions. Economic conditions are anticipated as favorable when an economy is expanding and not favorable when an economy is contracting. Also, it is known that ex-post realizations of credit problems show procyclical markings, and they would increase in times of recessions and decrease during expansion. But these markings may behave in the same way with fixed portfolio loss distributions which have no systematic risk factors in either the failure probabilities or the loss given default (Allen and Saunders, 2004).

The term "procyclicality" is described by Kaminsky, Reinhart and Vegh (2004) with the phenomenon "*When it rains, it pours*". They argue that macroeconomic policies are highly procyclical, especially during times of high risk and so are more dangerous than during ordinary times of the economy. In an emerging economy such as Turkey, fiscal authorities typically reduce budget deficits while the central bank moves interest rates to a higher level, and this probably makes the bad situation worse. However, cyclical policies do not exist only in the crisis periods in many emerging economies. Some of the most basic features of debt crises in emerging economies include high spending and borrowing during the periods when the economy is expanding and international capital is abundant. In connection with this, determination of appropriate capital has been discussed for many years and capital adequacy requirements have been found to be the most effective instrument to protect financial institutions from risks. Basel II accord includes many aspects to bring capital charges into use for individual loans that are decided upon by model-based estimates from banks internal risk models. But the way in which capital charges and asset risk are related to each other may exacerbate procyclicality. In case that asset risks are determined by looking at economic conditions, there will be a rise in the amount of capital requirement during a downturn and bank capital is likely to be gradually destroyed by loan write-offs. Banks that have limited capital cannot raise new equity easily during downturn and this situation will make the banks move into deleveraging by decreasing lending, and that makes the conditions worse (Behn, et al., 2016, pp. 919–920).

Some other researchers define the procyclicality as a source of economic recession, which navigate financial crisis deepen (Kalemli-Ozcan and Sorensen, 2011). In their study, Claessens, Ghosh, and Mihet (2014) refer to a system as procyclical if the system increases the effects of the business cycle or strengthens it. They state that in a procyclical system, the financial institutions and financial markets move in the same direction. When there is a positive shock, asset prices and credits increase and this condition promotes an increase in economic activity. On the other hand, if the cycle moves in the opposite direction, then asset prices and credits decline and in connection with this situation, economic activities become slower. A similar definition can be seen in the study of Baglioni, et al. (2012). They also point out that asset growth will lead to collateral growth and thus credit growth, which in turn will create cyclical upturns. In this case, the financial system has an amplification effect on the business cycle. In the opposite case, the amplification mechanism does not work because of the unfavorable effect of monetary policy on banks' balance sheets.

European Central Bank (ECB) (2005) also makes a similar definition to all these definitions and mention that the banks' loan moves in the same direction that the real economy is moving. Therefore, economic growth triggers loan growth, and economic contraction causes loan declines.

As seen above, procyclicality has been defined in many ways by many researchers, authors and institutions. Although there are still discussions about the causes of procyclicality, the most accepted ones will be provided in detail in the forthcoming subsection.

2.2 Causes of procyclicality

Several factors contribute to the procyclical behavior of the financial sector. Among these, the following are most well-known: Deviations from the Efficient Market Hypothesis, Credit Rating Agencies, Economic Policy, Basel II, Fair Value Accounting and Leverage. Detailed information about all of them is given below.

2.2.1 Deviations from the efficient market hypothesis

A market is efficient when prices reflect fully available information. Of course, there must be sufficient conditions for the market to be efficient. For example, there shouldn't be any transaction costs, available information should be costless to everyone and the implications of existing information for the existing price and distributions of future prices of each security should express the same opinion to everyone (Fama, 1969, p. 383). There are three types of markets under efficiency context. The weak form of efficient market reflects all previously available information to the market prices. As today's stock prices reflect all previous information, investors cannot estimate the future prices of stocks with technical analysis. On the other hand, there is still room for fundamental analysis, where price levels can be judged to determine undervalued and overvalued stocks which indeed give investors a chance of making abnormal profits. The second form of efficient market is semi-strong. In the semi-strong efficient market, current prices reflect all historical and all publicly available information such that investors cannot use either technical or fundamental analysis to obtain abnormal returns. In the strong form of the efficient market, all types of information, including the private (insider) information, are totally reflected in current stock prices. Therefore, there is no information that gives investors any advantage to get abnormal returns than the other investors on the market.

Efficient market hypothesis has asserted that everyone can reach all available information and can make sensible judgments, recognize and understand the difference between economic shocks and events with continued influence effect. In an efficient market, banks behave countercyclically and understand how serious the economy is and as a precaution, they lower (raise) their loans by raising (lower) loan interest rate. But banks begin to behave procyclical when there is a market imperfection (ECB, January-2005, p. 56).

Efficient market explains the cyclical/procyclical behavior by asymmetric information, principal-agent problems, herding, free-riding problems, moral hazard and disaster myopia (Athanasoglou, et al. 2013, pp. 60–61). As a market imperfection, asymmetric information, which is defined as informational differences between borrowers and lenders (Leland and Pyle, 1977, p. 371), is regarded as the main cause of procyclicality (ECB, January-2005). Banks give more loans during the upward phase of the cycle and think that the borrowers are less risky. On the other hand, they tighten their lending standards during the downward phase of the cycle and perceive the borrowers to be dangerous. As a result, the monitoring costs vary with the economic cycle and the underlying costs lead to fluctuations in the credit cycle (Athanasoglou, et al., 2013, p. 61). These informational differences have strong grounds for higher provisioning and at the same time lower profitability and dividends which send out negative signals to the market about the banks' financial condition (Rajan, 1994). Moreover, these negative signals make the bad economic conditions even worse.

The other market imperfection that may cause procyclicality is the principal-agent problem. It represents the conflict between shareholders and bank managers which may arise from different risk profiles or adverse selection phenomenon (Eisenhardt, 1989). This assumption causes procyclicality when systematic risk and instability is high and when managers take excessive risks for getting higher incentives from the principal. In this case, borrowers underestimate risk and continue to have the possibility for excess profits, but this gives rise to lenders losing their capital (Landau, 2009).

Additionally, it is believed that moral hazard problems cause procyclicality. Moral hazard which is a subjective dilemma arises when banks are declared "system-relevant" and cannot go bankrupt. The decision-makers of such banks do not play the game according to the rules. They can take more risk, with less equity and if the investment goes bankrupt, the states must be liable and provide funds for the rescue. The term "too big to fail" was shaped by this situation and means exactly that these institutions are too big to be allowed to go bankrupt. If one of these large banks decays, many more would follow. For this reason, the term "system-relevant" was also shaped. Such a bank, for example, is in a sense, full-free because nothing can happen to it. The moral hazard is an increased risk-taking behavior and causes deviation from efficient market (Athanasoglou, et al., 2013, p. 61).

Besides the moral hazard problems, disaster myopia also plays a dynamic role in procyclicality. According to Guttentag and Herring (1986), the behavior of a bank's management and borrowers is myopic, because they only consider short-term risks and relying on their previous experience, they assume that they will be able to cope with this kind of stagnation and do not seriously consider the possibility of highly unfavorable economic situations. And this is evidenced by the fact that experienced personnel are out of business, banks are less rigorous in credit standards or that stakeholders are less empowered to supervise the management and forget about the problems in the credit portfolio of the recent crisis.

Herding is another issue that should be considered while investigating the effect of market imperfections on cyclical behavior of banks. As also emphasized in the work of Rajan (2005), bank's management and large institutional investors make their business in the way that their competitors do and this behavior increases the market volatility. This is mainly a result of the integrity of information and technology, which can accelerate sudden changes in market liquidity and these changes are accepted to have a contribution for making price fluctuations in some cases stronger (Athanasoglou and Daniilidis 2011, p. 15).

2.2.2 Credit rating agencies

Credit rating can be defined as an evaluation of the creditworthiness. It reflects the ability of a company to meet the contractual obligations in a full and timely manner. It refers to the assessment of corporate loyalty. However, ratings can also be directly related to a single issue or bank borrower and therefore do not include an assessment of the general creditworthiness, but instead assess the risk of the borrower's default payments for the individual issue or bank liability. The rating judgment on the credit quality of the debtor is expressed in the form of letters, numbers and / or symbol combinations, so-called rating symbols (like "AAA", "AA1" or "AA -"). Each of these rating symbols denotes a risk class, so that a company will be assigned by the credit assessment of a risk or rating category and each of them includes various pieces of information such as average default probability and volatility of the default probability, which are identical for each borrower in the corresponding risk class. External rating agencies have the task of classifying borrowers into a corresponding risk class according to several quantitative and qualitative factors. In accordance with the risk class, the minimum capital requirement is allocated. The better the assigned risk class of the potential borrower, the lower the probability of default and thus the minimum capital required for the credit.

Rating assessments of external rating agencies have the aim, of presenting the creditworthiness of companies in a clear and accurate manner, taking into account current factors. The rating judgment has the function of ensuring market transparency and thus the efficiency of the financial markets, and to serve potential investors as an indicator of the future viability of a company or person. The characteristics of the creditworthiness rating and the reliability of ratings can therefore be regarded as fulfilled. Criticism, however, is the timeliness of ratings, which does not always seem to be given. Often, it is only after an obvious deterioration in the creditworthiness of a company that the rating agency is adjusted. The rating reveals the deterioration in creditworthiness that has already occurred and thus partly loses its function as an indicator of the future viability of the company. An early detection of insolvencies based on external ratings is thus not necessarily possible.

On the other hand, for financial firms, there are two main rating approaches which explain bank portfolio credit risk. One of them is "Point in Time" and the other approach is "Through the Cycle". Point in Time rating system generates a probability default rate that is countercyclical and related to short run macroeconomic conditions. It is a sign that probability default rate will increase during recessions and decrease during expansions. Although it is known that Point in Time approach strengthens the procyclicality of financial system, there is not any certain clarification from what perspective a rating system should be used in calculating probability default other than this method. In Basel accords and Euro-system credit assessment framework, both of these rating approaches are permitted to be used. On the other hand, the Cycle rating approach generates a more straight probability default rate giving attention to removing the cyclical factors which indicate a long-run credit risk profile, and a stable and less-volatile financial system (Cesaroni, 2015, p. 63). The rating agencies should see "Through the Cycle" (Hahn, 2002). As discussed in Standard & Poor's report (2002, p. 41) *"The ideal is to rate "through the cycle". There is no point in assigning high ratings to a company enjoying peak prosperity if that performance level is expected to be only temporary. Similarly, there is no need to lower ratings to reflect poor performance as long as one can reliably anticipate that better times are just around the corner."* but it should be kept in mind that the calculation of the failure rates also has a cyclic pattern.

As also emphasized in the work of Amato and Furfine (2003), the financial system is procyclical and the amount of financial activities rise further during economic booms and decrease during recessions. Economic development at high level causes an increase in values of potential collateral, by that making credit constraints less tight and make it simple to reach debt financing. In their study, Altman and Kao (1992, pp. 64–75) clarify how the correlation of default probabilities, loss in case of default and the business cycle behave towards each other. They concluded that during economic downturns the models which accept independence of default probabilities and loss given default would likely guess the probability of severe loss lower than it really is. In another study, Bangia, Diebold and Schuermann (2000) prove the procyclicality of credit character becomes different by comparing the estimated credit losses in contraction and expansion period. They find that the estimated credit losses are much higher in a contraction period relative to an expansion. The comprehensive study of Amato and Furfine (2003) emphasize that almost all the time, ratings do not change and rating agencies carefully watch and check the conditions of firms in order to see how they change over a period of time, and in most cases, do not respond to small changes in the risk characteristic of firms. But, when rating agencies make any changes, their response is an overreaction and the natural tendency of this overreaction is closely connected with the condition of the economy. Excessive state of having positive beliefs (negative beliefs) during upturns (downturns) of rating agencies could be the reason for this situation.

2.2.3 Economic policy

Fiscal and monetary policies have an effect on banks procyclical behavior. In reality, fiscal policies have to be countercyclical for balance of the economy. For example, during a recession, decision-makers can lower taxes or increase government spending to increase aggregate demand and force overall economy for recovery. But there are some situations that fiscal policies cannot help for economic improvement, which means sometimes fiscal policies can be procyclical instead of being countercyclical (Athanasoglou and Daniilidis, 2011, p. 17). This is usually the case in underdeveloped countries. In their study, Cuadra, Sanchez and Sapriza (2009) found that in developed countries, fiscal policy is countercyclical and is not affected by economic cycles. On the other hand, it is procyclical in emerging countries, and in a recession they must deal with higher costs while financing their public sector. These higher costs make their banks to increase lending interest rates and reduce loan supply, which causes procyclicality.

Monetary policy is another contributing factor in procyclicality (ECB, 2009, pp. 63–80). It causes procyclicality due to the following reasons:

- it is related with interest rate which affects loan demand,
- it is related with credit channel which affects the cost of funding and the banks' capital base and borrowers' property and collateral value,
- and lastly, it is related with the risk-taking channel (Borio and Zhu, 2008).

Measures on procyclicality are closely linked to the macroeconomic stabilization policies. A more resilient financial system complements anti-cyclical monetary and fiscal policy and contributes to countering the dangers to financial stability in the downturn. For its part, monetary policy must be more strongly opposed to the development of systemic risks in the financial sector during the boom phase. This can be achieved with extension of time horizons, which would also promote price stability in the long term more effectively.

2.2.4 Basel II and procyclicality

In view of globalized capital markets, there is a need for internationally agreed rules for credit institutions. The 1988 Basel Accord was published as a first world standard for the equity requirements of credit institutions by the Basel Committee on Banking Supervision. The objective of the Basel Committee on Banking Supervision of 1988 was to increase the stability of the financial markets. As indicated in Table 2.1, Basel I includes two base capital classes, which are Tier 1 and Tier 2 capital. Tier 1 capital contains paid-up capital and reserves. On the other hand, Tier 2 capital restrict Tier 1 capital within certain limits of a maximum 100 percent and includes undisclosed reserves, asset valuation reserves, general provisions, hybrid instruments and subordinated debt (Balthazar, 2006,18).

Table 2.1: Description of Capital

Tier 1	- Paid-up capital
	- Disclosed reserves (retained profits, legal reserves)
Tier 2	- Undisclosed reserves
	- Asset revaluation reserves
	- General provisions
	- Hybrid provisions (must be unsecured, fully paid-up)
	- Subordinated debt (max. 50% Tier 1, min. 5 years- discount factor for shorter maturities)
Deductions	- Goodwill (from Tier 1)
	- Investments in unconsolidated subsidiaries (from Tier 1 and Tier 2)

Source: Balthazar, 2006, p. 18.

After determination of capital, the risk weight was classified into 5 categories namely, 0%, 0% to 50%, 20, 50%, 100%. The Table 2.2 below depicts the list of risk weight of assets. The 0% risk category consists of cash, central bank and government debt, Organization for Economic Co-operation and Development (OECD) central governments and other central government debts, which are expressed and funded in the local currency. The 20 % risk category is made up of OECD and multilateral development banks debt, non-OECD bank debt, which has less than one year of maturity and OECD public sector debt. Mortgages are in the 50% category, and all other claims like private sector debt and non-OECD bank debt which have a maturity of more than one year are included in the 100% category.

Table 2.2: Risk Weight of Assets

%	**Item**
0	- cash
	- claims on OECD central governments
	- claims on other central governments if they are denominated and funded in the national currency (to avoid country transfer risk)
20	- claims on OECD banks and multilateral development banks
	- claims on banks outside OECD with residual maturity < 1 year
	- claims on public sector entities of OECD countries
50	- mortgage loans
100	- all other claims: claims on corporate, claims on banks outside OECD with a maturity > 1 year, fixed assets, all other assets

Source: Balthazar, 2006, p. 19.

At the heart of the debate was the main risk, namely the credit risk. In this context, a minimum required capital ratio of 8 percent of the issued credit volume has been provided. In 1996, the concept was supplemented by the market risk. However, developments in the banking sector have shown that the Basel Committee on Banking Supervision in 1988 was far from the actual target. The shortcomings of Basel I accord are as follows (Federal Reserve Bulletin, September 2003, pp. 396–397):

- It was very simple, but tried to solve complex banking problems.
- There was inadequate differentiation among degrees of risk, which added misleading news about a bank's capital adequacy compared to its risk.
- For big banks, Basel I ratio didn't indicate the risk adequately and judge bank strength correctly.

For these shortcomings, new measures had to be taken to ensure the stability of the financial markets. The revision of the old accord by the Basel Committee on the concept of Basel II aims to achieve the security and soundness of the financial sector by a more comprehensive and risk-adequate coverage ratio of major banking risks through compliant, flexible and theoretically feasible regulations.

Figure 2.1: Proposed changes to elements of the capital ratio under Basel II

$$\frac{\begin{array}{c}\textit{Regulatory capital}\\ \textit{(Definition unchanged)}\end{array}}{\begin{array}{c}\textit{Measure of risk exposure}\\ \textit{(Risk − weighted assets)}\\ \textit{(Measure revised)}\end{array}} = \begin{array}{c}\textit{Minimum required}\\ \textit{capital ratio}\\ \textit{(\%8 minimum unchanged)}\end{array}$$

↓

Credit risk exposure (Measure revised)	+	Market risk exposure (Measure unchanged)	+	Operational risk exposure (Explicit measure added)

Source: Federal Reserve Bulletin, September 2003, p. 398.

There are three Pillars of Basel II accord. The first pillar focuses on the minimum capital requirements for credit, market and operational risks, and expands the rules introduced by Basel I accord. The definition of regulatory capital remains unchanged, so the minimum capital requirement, which is at least 8% of risk-weighted assets, stays the same. Figure 2.1 shows the changes made with Basel II. The second pillar focuses on the problems of banking verification supervisory procedures. The aim is to provide information through various measures as well as to support the supervisory authorities. This allows the supervisory authorities to increase or reduce the minimum capital requirements with the aim of counteracting the procyclical impact of the capital requirements. The last pillar of Basel II is about market discipline. Banks must provide information on the application of capital requirements, equity structure, the structure and extent of the risks incurred (credit risk, operational risk and market risk) and the adequacy of equity capital. These measures are expected to increase the transparency of banking activities. This would lead to increased market pressure and competition, as the banks' own initiatives would ensure an adequate risk structure and credit conditions (ECB, January 2005, p. 52).

On the condition of determining risk weights according to Basel II's Standardized Approach, the external ratings are considered through the cycle and this gives rise to cyclicality. On the other hand, the cyclicality caused from Internal Ratings-Based Approach (IRB) is related to capital requirements. There are three fundamental risk components in IRB, which are the probability of default, loss given default and exposure at default. Cyclical movements impact these risk components and affect banks' capital requirements. Pillar 1 furthers the progress of risk components using as a basis of "*ideally cover at least one economic cycle*" and the action of confirming must be related with the data that maintain at least one business cycle. For example, a stress test must include scenarios that are based on economic downturns and consider recessions to specify the effects on the bank's risk coefficients (Novoa, Scarlata, and Sole, 2009, p. 12).

The tendency to procyclical behavior of the financial sector has been investigated for some time. The presumption of a procyclical effect of Basel II in this context is based on the following mechanism. One of the most important concepts of Basel II is the calculation of default probabilities for loans. Since this magnitude correlates strongly with cyclical factors, these probabilities change after the cyclical cycle. This means that in the expansion and boom phases, the probability of failure decreases, while it increases markedly in a recession and depression phase. This situation means that credit institutions need a higher capital requirement in the economic downturn than during an economic upturn. This change in the equity ratio affects the volume of loans that are potentially to be issued. As a result, banks have fewer funds available for the granting of loans in the economic downturn. This reduction in loans also means a reduction in financing possibilities for companies and households. In addition, consumption and investment activity are restricted, which ultimately restricts economic growth.

According to the Financial System Review of the Bank of Canada, the problem begins when risk changes with time based on economic and financial conditions. In the time of economic growth, predicted possibilities of default are likely to decline, which provide lower minimum capital requirements per unit of risk-weighted assets according to Basel II accord. This capital support brings out favorable circumstances for banks to grow their supply of loans during the economic cycle when lending conditions are simple and asset prices increase quickly. In this condition, banks use this larger amount of capital for maximizing the return to its shareholders. This situation causes an increase in macro-prudential risk. In other words, the consequently higher leverage in the banking sector could increase the effect of an economic or financial shock while the capital of banks become insufficient for managing the unanticipated loan losses and asset write-downs that occur with the shock. Furthermore, issues related to increased default risk make a connection with an economic downturn will also increase minimum capital requirement under Basel II, and this makes the situation worse (Bank of Canada: Financial System Review, June 2009, p. 34).

Another study of the Financial Stability Review, discussing the degree of procyclicality of Basel II accord, claims that Basel II may raise the volatility of bank capital requirements over the business cycle. As shown in Figure 2.2 below, when the economy is going well, there is lower capital needs for the identical risk exposure, an increase in the credit supply and further revival in the economy. Whereas during the opposite situation, when there is a period in which business activity and production is reduced and conditions become worse, credit risk that measured by probability of default and loss given default would to increase. Further, the capital requirements would be increased and banks would deal with higher capital requirement with the same time that there is a decrease in their profits which arise from the write-offs on defaulted loans. When higher capital requirement and low supply of new capital exist together, it increases the effect of the downturn (ECB Financial Stability Review, December 2009, p. 1439).

Figure 2.2: The procyclicality effects of risk-sensitive regulatory capital

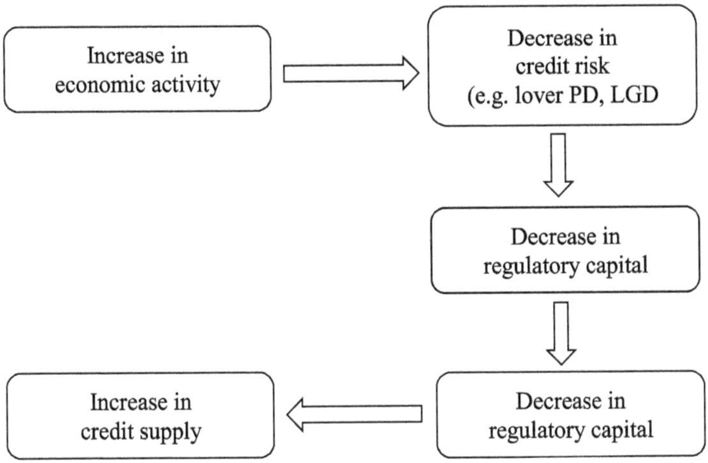

Source: ECB Financial Stability Review, December 2009, p. 1439.

In 2010, the central banks and supervisory authorities of the most financially strong countries have set new capital rules through the Basel Committee on Banking Supervision, Basel III, in order to counter bank rescue operations after the financial crisis in 2007 and to further strengthen financial systems.

2.2.5 Fair value accounting

FAS 157 defines fair value as "*the price that would be received to sell an asset or paid to transfer a liability in an orderly transaction between market participants at the measurement date.*" (Statement of Financial Accounting Standards, 2006, p. 2). Here an "orderly transaction" intend to a transaction that made voluntarily and relaxed. In addition, "at the measurement date" has a meaning of indicating the conditions that exist at the balance sheet date. And if we combine them, "at the measurement date" and "orderly transaction" together mean that the prediction of the price at which the transaction occurs at a future date should be based on the information being used now and reflect current market conditions (Ryan, 2008, p. 26).

The fair value measurement standard defines a hierarchy that is based on the observability of the valuation criteria in the market. This is intended to ensure the information on the market is kept in the balance sheet. In this context, a fair value hierarchy is taken into account in the context of IFRS 13 with regard to the treatment of financial instruments. This provides a three-level fair value hierarchy (Statement of Financial Accounting Standards, 2006, pp. 26–28):

Level 1: Financial instruments whose market prices are known in the active market. These are financial instruments whose fair value can be directly derived from prices in liquid markets.

Level 2: Financial instruments that are measured with valuation procedures that are on the basis of observable market data. These are financial instruments whose fair value can be determined from similar financial instruments traded in active markets.

Level 3: Financial instruments that are measured with valuation procedures that are on the basis of unobservable parameters. These are financial instruments whose fair value cannot be determined from observable market data and require a different evaluation procedure.

The characteristics of each level are summarized in Table 2.3.

Table 2.3: Features of Each Level in the Fair Value Hierarchy

Level	Characteristics
1	Observable Quoted prices for identical assets or liabilities in active markets (unadjusted)
2	Quoted prices for similar items in active markets Quoted prices for identical/ similar items, no active market Liabilities traded as assets in inactive markets
3	Unobservable inputs (e.g., a reporting entity's or other entity's own data) Market participant (not entity-specific) perspective is still required

Source: PWC Fair Value Measurements, 2005, pp. 4–34.

Accounting for financial instruments at fair value has been strongly criticized after the 2007 crisis. Critics accuse the fair value accounting (FVA) as being procyclical and therefore exacerbating the financial market crisis. In normal market conditions, the fair value accounting does not have a procyclical effect, but only reflects the expectations of the respective market participant. In the abnormal market situation, the valuation is difficult. As there are no suitable market values, valuation models have to be applied. The criticism is partly based on a market situation in which there is no more price formation. For example, the price at an emergency sale is not a market price, because it is not a fair value to which an asset can be evaluated with an objective consideration of its real value.

Barth (1994) examined whether disclosed fair values of banks' investment securities and fair value securities gains and losses are a sign of share prices compared with historical costs, in order to show which is more appropriate and reliable to investors for valuing banks' equity. As a result of the study, it is determined that the fair value of investment securities have more explanatory influence beyond historical cost. Additionally, Barth, Landsman, and Wahlen (1995) made a study and tried to find how fair value accounting influences suddenly changes in earnings and either there is any incremental volatility observed in bank share prices. They used a sample of annual data from 1971–1990 for US banks and chose historical cost net income, historical cost net income plus unrealized annual gains and losses (fair value net income), realized securities gains and losses and unrealized securities gains and losses as earnings variables. They found that fair value–based earnings are more volatile than historical cost earnings, in spite of the fact that share prices do not show any sudden change.

According to Novoa, Scarlata and Sole (2009), although fair value accounting has an unintended procyclical effect, it is continuing to be used by financial institutions. They find out that the application of fair value accounting causes undesirable volatility and complexity in measurement. In addition, this complexity does not come into being during identifying Future Value of prices in recessions and illiquid markets, further during good times and in liquid markets when prices increase and include risk premium that exaggerate profits. In case of such situations, market prices may not exactly reflect risks and can follow as the consequence of extreme profits that give a misleading or false impression of incentives and increase the cyclical upturn. Focusing on the weaknesses of FVA, they suggest that capital buffers, forward-looking provisioning and disclosures that unwanted elements having been removed by processing can reduce the procyclicality of FVA.

Based on the evidence provided in the comprehensive study of Broden and Olovsson (2011), the fair value accounting has a procyclical effect on Swedish banking sector. Furthermore, they contend that the contribution of fair value accounting to the banks' earnings change among the banks and the general mood of financial markets. On the condition that total asset values of banks rise, they are likely to increase their leverage ratios during the recovery phase in the business cycle. Thus, the Swedish banks do actively manage their balance sheets and change their leverage ratios. They do not have an exact leverage ratio, but they increase their leverage ratio when the economy is good and total asset rise and as a result provide procyclicality. On the other hand, focusing on the contribution of bank regulation and fair value accounting to procyclical leverage, Zadeh, et al., (2015) find out based on a large sample of US commercial banks that bank regulation contributes to procyclical leverage but fair value accounting does not have any effect. They used three experiments to measure the extent to which fair value accounting contribute procyclical leverage. First, they analyzed the relation between change in leverage and change in assets and included fair value comprehensive income as an independent variable into the model. Second, they expanded this analysis and added the interaction between the measure of fair value comprehensive income and the banks' net purchases of assets. And lastly, they looked at the relationship between change in leverage and change in assets, disaggregating change in assets into fair value comprehensive income, change in equity other than that is based on the comprehensive income, change in debt, and other changes in assets. Whereas they found that bank regulation contributes to procyclical leverage, they could not find any proof that fair value accounting contributes to procyclical leverage. In a study similar to this one, Laux and Rauter (2016) argue that leverage is strongly procyclical. But, they do not find any evidence that fair value accounting increases procyclical leverage and historical cost accounting decreases the procyclicality. Taking everything into account, the business model of banks and the amount of the regulatory capital and leverage ratio have more effect on the procyclical leverage than fair value accounting or banks regulatory risk weights.

2.2.6 Leverage

The leverage ratio shows the degree of indebtedness of a company. The leverage effect plays an important role in strengthening economic cycles. The market participants manage their balance sheets more or less actively on the basis of the price and risk changes. If market-wide changes occur simultaneously, this results in a synchronized action by the market participants. An increased demand for securities with the same supply can trigger an increase in prices during the boom period. The balance sheet increases due to the increase in the value of the assets and the equity increases as a residual value. If a constant leverage ratio is assumed, the absolute debt can be increased. On the other hand, the balance sheets are shrinking in times of recession, since the assets which measured at fair value are at a lower level and equity decreases as a residual value. In the case of a constant leverage ratio, the bank must either sell assets or increase equity. As it is known that capital procurement is difficult during the crisis periods, the bank chose selling their assets. As a result, the prices of the securities are further reduced so that securities must again be sold until the constant leverage ratio is reached. The leverage ratio often behaves procyclically, which means that the leverage ratio increases during periods of boom and conversely, it falls during the recession. For the United States, Adrian and Shin (2010) show that marked-to-market leverage is strongly procyclical – that is, an increase in debt levels in phases of economic development – was particularly evident among the large US investment banks. This is different for the commercial banks, which have a substantially constant leverage over the cycle, mainly because they are subject to banking regulations. They show the relationship between balance sheet size and leverage for a household in a simple example. According to this example, a household buys a house that is funded by a mortgage. And they suppose that the house is worth 100, the mortgage value is 90, and the household has a net worth of equity 10. Then the existing balance sheet looks like:

Assets		Liabilities	
House	100	Equity	10
		Mortgage	90

Leverage can be calculated from the formula of total assets to total equity and get a value of 10 (100/10). Assume that there is a fluctuation in asset price and the price of securities increases by 1% and asset value becomes 101. The debt stays constant at 90 and then total leverage is:

$$L = A/(A - 90)$$

Assets		Liabilities	
House	101	Equity	11
		Mortgage	90

If the price of the house increases, then the net worth of asset increases, and the leverage ratio becomes smaller due to the negative relationship between leverage and total asset.

If we consider how the change in the structure of financial institutions such as banks came about, we can see that banks behave in a different way. In the first case, the bank's balance sheet looks like the following.

Assets		Liabilities	
Securities	100	Equity	10
		Debt	90

Think that the price of debt does not become different for little changes in total assets. Let's think that the price of securities becomes bigger by 1% to 101.

Assets		Liabilities	
Securities	101	Equity	11
		Debt	90

If the financial intermediary manages its balance sheet actively to keep a constant leverage ratio of 10, then leverage ratio will decrease to 9.18 (101/11). If the bank targets a leverage of 10, it should take additional debt to purchase new securities and total debt becomes 99. Consequently, 1 unit increase in the price of assets causes an increase in debt by 9 unit.

$$\frac{\text{assets}}{\text{equity}} = \frac{101 + D}{11} = 10$$

The leverage is 10 again, after the increase in debt.

Assets		Liabilities	
Securities	110	Equity	11
		Debt	99

For the opposite case assume that there is recession in the economy and the security price decrease to 109. Then there will be a decrease in liabilities side, too. Because the value of debt remains almost constant, the equity will be 10.

Assets		Liabilities	
Securities	109	Equity	10
		Debt	99

Now the leverage ratio is 109/10= 10.9 and it is higher than the targeted value. The high leverage can be decreased by selling securities worth by 9, and the debt drops by 9. Then the new balance sheet looks as follows. Eventually, the balance sheet returns to where it started before the price changed and the leverage returns to the target level.

Assets		Liabilities	
Securities	100	Equity	10
		Debt	90

As seen in Figure 2.3, when there is high demand for an asset, then the price of it tends to increase, and this causes a feedback effect in which strong balance sheets lead to higher demand for the asset and this situation increases the asset's price again and makes the balance sheet stronger. The figure below shows leverage adjustment in upturn and downturn periods. In the opposite case when markets are not perfectly liquid, then the price of an asset decreases, and this is the reason for a weak balance sheet which promotes more sales of the asset that reduces the price of the asset and makes the balance sheet weaker.

Figure 2.3: Leverage adjustment in upturn and downturn

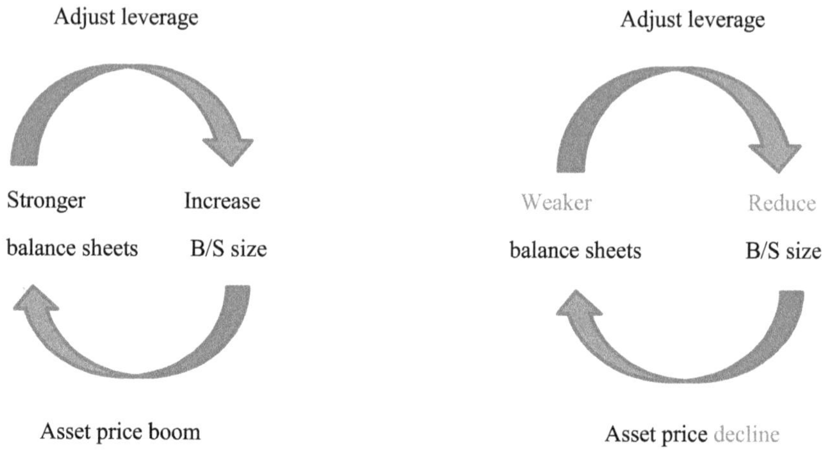

Source: Adrian and Shin, 2010, p. 424.

With reference to banks specific and macroeconomic determinants of banks' leverage, Giordana and Schumacher (2012) focus on the procyclicality of leverage for Luxembourg banks to evaluate the pre-crisis and crisis period using individual bank level data that covers 2003 Q1–2010 Q1 periods. They define leverage ratio as *"how much of a bank's own fund covers its assets, which is indicative for the level of indebtedness of a bank."* The level of indebtedness is determined by the banks' willingness to take risks, the evaluation of economic conditions and general scale of demand in the economy. The aim of their study is to determine the connection between the changes in leverage decisions and balance sheet components. Their findings show that the leverage of Luxembourg's bank that are liquidity providers to the European banking sector are highly procyclical and expand their balance sheet when the spread of Euribor-OIS increases. There are four reasons for the significant correlation between growth in leverage and growth in asset for most of the banks in Luxembourg. First reason is the active management of balance sheet that means the Luxembourg's banks borrow more when economic conditions are good and raise their assets and on the other hand, when something goes wrong in the economy they reduce their assets. Secondly, most of the banks in Luxembourg are branches or subsidiaries and they need to be protected by their mother companies. As a result of this protection, their leverage becomes the highest leverage in Europe which creates a target level for leverage. Thirdly, the reason for the cyclical behavior of Luxembourg's banks is based on the Euribor-OIS spread which makes the funding on the European interbank market more price, and this condition forces mother companies or groups to demand additional credits from their Luxembourgish branches and subsidiaries. And lastly, the expansion in security prices makes them draw attention, and they find that banks increase their holdings of securities provide funding through more deposits that encourage a growth in leverage.

Kalemli-Ozcan, Sorensen and Yesiltas (2012 argue for the existence of leverage procyclicality for large commercial banks located in the United States, but to a smaller degree in comparison to European banks. Because increasing leverage before the crisis period gave commercial banks an advantage with regard to raising funds in the short term and to using off-balance sheet items to avoid capital requirements, they took excessive risk in reliance on explicit deposit insurance and implicit insurance which require earnest legal regulation. Laux and Rauter (2016) also share the same view in that understanding the determinants of procyclical leverage is crucial for recognition of possible problems which arise from reporting, regulation and management. As part of their study, they focus on the determinants of leverage procyclicality for US commercial and savings banks and blame the difference between regulatory risk weights and changes in average risk weights. Despite controlling various economic and bank-specific variables, they discover that banks' leverage is strongly procyclical, not only because of the fair value accounting but also because of the adjustment of the balance sheet. Some of the determinants that are key drivers of procyclicality are listed by the same authors as GDP (Gross Domestic Product) growth, gains on loan sales and average risk weights.

Even though leverage procyclicality is a significant topic studied in numerous areas of academic literature during the last few decades, a specific definition has not yet been accepted. Geanakoplos (2010) explained the anatomy of cyclical leverage for the business sector:

- Asset value decreases with bad news.
- That gives rise to a decrease in the wealth of the natural buyers (which is defined as optimists) that were leveraged and these bad news force leveraged buyers to sell their assets to compensate their marginal requirement.

- This sale causes further loss in asset values and in the wealth of optimists.
- Owing to high instability in market, margin requirements become tighter.
- This makes big losses in asset values by necessary sales.
- Most of the natural buyers lose their whole wealth and quit.
- Bad news can cause spreading effect and optimists may sell all the other assets.

Consequently, Geanakoplos (2010) claims that procyclical leverage is based on three main elements which feed back on each other. Basic element is the bad news which increases the uncertainty in asset values. This uncertainty makes the lenders nervous and causes strict margins. And finally, this causes a decline in asset prices and big losses by leveraged buyers.

According to the report prepared by Bank for International Settlements (2014), excess leverage, which is defined as the extent to which a business funds its assets with borrowings instead of equity, can cause problems. These problems can mainly arise from fixed obligations which may not be fulfilled during economic recessions because the generated cash flow by a firm's asset level may be very low during these times. The leverage ratio in the banking sector is typically higher than in other sectors and this high level of leverage can pose a risk to the entire economic system, potentially affecting the welfare and steadiness of economy. Determining the optimal level of leverage helps to control the leverage risk which can be maintained with risk-based capital adequacy ratios that ascertain the degree of banks' capital relative to the risk of its business activities. As we will also argue later, we can summarize the basic rule as "the more risk, the more capital required balancing it." Hardouvelis (2010) argue that we need to know very well what causes procyclicality for taking measures against it. He classifies the reasons into five categories. The first category is factors that are around the economic environment like globalization, technological improvements, short-termism – which is the behavior of firms' managers who are not forward-looking – and inertia in household and business sentiment. The second category includes the factors related to the financial environment such as the similarity of techniques and data, determinants of risk management, similarity in the behaviors of fund managers and the behavior of rating agencies. Thirdly, factors related to economic policymakers are listed. Political pressure, the behavior of policymakers, and bias of policymakers are the cause of financial system cyclicality. In fourth place, there are the factors related to the nature of the financial system, i.e., the Basel II accord and capital adequacy, bank provisioning, mark to market accounting, leverage, liquidity, collateral requirements and margin requirement, interconnectedness, home vs. host country regulations, and market structure and organization. The final category includes the design of regulatory instruments that may prevent procyclicality in the financial system. These are the set of instruments such as regulatory policies, comprehensive regulations, countercyclical and trigger mechanisms, choice of regulators, timing, and cost of regulation. Leverage that is classified in the fourth category is blamed to cause procyclical financial system because of not being simple and transparent and can be manipulated and circumvented easily.

Several important implications of Baglioni, et al., (2012)'s study are worth emphasizing. By analyzing a sample of 77 banks from 18 European countries, they tried to find out whether there is a procyclical behavior in the banks of Eastern, Western and Atlantic countries. According to their results, most of the European investment banks have procyclical leverage and this cyclicality has negative consequences on the economy and on the stability of financial system. This unpleasant situation can be prevented by relying on monetary policy with prudential measures such as regulatory limits to the leverage ratio.

The relationship between leverage and economic conditions has been examined by many economists in the international arena with different approaches and methods. However, the literature related to cyclical leverage practices in Turkey received little attention. One prominent study conducted by Binici and Köksal (2012) that investigates the connection between the leverage of Turkish banks and asset growth for the period December 2002 and August 2011 and argues that banks provide money for their activities by means of equity and debt, and if leverage is the ratio of assets to equity, then any modification in the value of assets will affect the value of equity, and hence there will be a change in leverage. For an economic agent, when the amount of debt remains constant, a rise in the amount of asset prices would decrease leverage, which is accepted as countercyclical leverage; this situation, however, is different for banks. Financial institutions, which have a target leverage level, use active leverage policy, where their leverage ratio changes according to the change in the market value of assets and equity.

The positive relationship between asset growth and leverage obtained from the study shows that leverage rises when there is active growth, which is evidence for the existence of procyclicality. In another recent study, Çalışkan (2011) tried to find out how Turkish financial system was not affected by the global financial crisis by making a comparison with the US financial system. As a result of bank-level panel regression analysis that covers 1994–2009 period, the leverage of Turkish banks is found to be procyclical; it increases (decreases) when there is a growth (decline) in balance sheets. The implication is that the regulatory and supervisory reforms that were implemented in Turkey after the 2001 financial crisis helped Turkish banks to avoid large leverage growth during the US financial crisis.

The overall interaction among leverage and procyclicality with a perspective of bank leverage increases the financial system cyclicality. As can be seen from the literature provided above, bank leverage typically rises during boom periods and falls during busts, so it can be said that leverage is procyclical. The expansion and contraction of balance sheet increase the volume of cyclicality. Therefore, banks should pay attention to their borrowing and lending attitudes. To decrease procyclicality, they should limit the increase in their leverage which could be particularly provided with a long-term target level, by setting a floor on the leverage ratio during economic growth. Alternatively, there could be an established process by which during downturns the limit is relaxed because the constant leverage ratio could amplify procyclicality by making deleverage during a downturn more likely to exist (D'Hulster, World Bank, 2009).

As it is seen, cyclical behavior of leverage has important outcomes for both the financial and real sector. The above-mentioned studies have examined leverage behavior with different approaches and methods. The following Table 2.4 summarizes these studies.

Table 2.4: A List of Empirical Studies in Literature

Study	Research Question	Dependent Variable(s)	Independent Variable(s)	Sample	Methodology
Adrian and Schin (2010)	Examining liquidity and leverage	- Leverage ratio $(\frac{Total\ Asset}{Total\ Equity})$	- Total assets (quarterly growth) - Repos (quarterly growth) - Trading VaR (quarterly growth, lag)	Five major US investment banks between the period 1997Q1–2008Q1	Panel data regression
Çalışkan (2011)	Leverage behavior of Turkish banks: How did they escape the global crisis?	- Leverage ratio $(\frac{Total\ Asset}{Total\ Equity})$	- Asset growth - CPI	Turkish banks and US banks between the period 1994–2009	Panel data regression
Broden and Olovsson (2011)	Investigating the fair value accounting and procyclical behaviour in the Swedish banking sector	- Δ Leverage $(\frac{\Delta Total\ Asset}{\Delta Total\ Equity})$	- Δ Total assets	Linear Regression	Big four Swedish banks between the period 2001–2010
Kalemli-Ozcan, et al. (2011)	Investigating the leverage across firms, banks and countries	- Leverage ratio $(1 - (\frac{equity}{asset}))$	- Size - Profit - Collateral	7334 US banks, 1123 European banks between 1990–2010	Panel data regression
Binici and Köksal (2012)	Is the leverage of Turkish banks procyclical?	- Debt / Equity - (Debt+Off Balance Sheet Liabilities) / Equity - Assets / Equity - (Tier 1 Capital-Regulatory Deductions) / (Assets+Off Balance Sheet Liabilities) - (Tier 1 Capital-Regulatory Deductions) / (Debt+Off Balance Sheet Liabilities) - [Assets + Contingencies + Commitments (except derivatives and revocables)] / Regulatory Capital	- Asset growth	Turkish banks between the period December 2002–August 2011	OLS
Baglioni, et al. (2012)	Is the leverage of European banks procyclical?	- Δ Leverage 1: (total assets/total equities) - Δ Leverage 2: (risk-weighted assets/ total regulatory capital) - Δ Leverage 3: (assets/ total regulatory capital)	- Δ Assets	A sample of 77 listed banks operating in 18 European countries over the period 2000–2009	Panel data regression
Giordana and Schumacher (2012)	What are the bank-specific and macroeconomic drivers of banks' leverage?	- Lagged growth in leverage $(\frac{Capital}{Asset})$	- Bank-specific variables - Macroeconomic conditions	- Luxembourg banks between 2003 Q1–2010 Q1	GMM

Study	Research Question	Dependent Variable(s)	Independent Variable(s)	Sample	Methodology
Beccalli, et al. (2015)	Examining leverage procyclicality and securitization in the US	- Δ Leverage $(\frac{Total\ Assets}{Bank\ Equity\ Capital})$	- Δ Assets - Dummy variable for securitizers banks - Positive distance of bank leverage capital requirement from the minimum leverage capital requirement - Negative distance of bank leverage capital requirement from the minimum leverage capital requirement - Δ Repos - Total capital ratio	US banks between 2001–2010	Two ways fixed effects panel data regression
Zadeh, et al. (2017)	The contribution of bank regulation and fair value accounting to procyclical leverage	- Δ Leverage $(\frac{Total\ Assets}{Total\ Equity})$	- Δ Assets - Δ Weighted average regulatory risk weight - Δ Non-risk-weighted assets - Δ Fair value comprehensive income deflated by lagged total assets - Net purchases of assets	A sample of 764 commercial banks between 2001 and 2013	Panel data regression
Laux and Rauter (2016)	Investigating the procyclicality of US bank leverage	- Δ Leverage $(\frac{Total\ Assets}{Total\ Equity})$	- Δ Total assets - Δ GDP - Δ VIX Volatility Index - Total Regulatory Capital Ratio - Δ Risk weights - Accounting items - Δ Goodwill	US commercial and saving banks between 1990–2013	Time Series Regression

3 The determinants of bank capital structure

3.1 Definition of capital structure

The question which factors determine capital structure and whether an optimal debt level exists is a central aspect of today's corporate finance research. For more than fifty years, scientists have been developing approaches to explain financing decisions. The irrelevance theory of Modigliani and Miller (1958) forms the foundation of modern capital structure research.

The capital structure can be seen from the liabilities side of the balance sheet and shows the extent to which the company is financed by equity and debt. Van Horne and Wachowicz (2008, p. 452) define capital structure as a mix of a firm's lasting long-term financing represented by debt, preferred stock and common stock equity. Debt indicates the borrowing money and must be repaid. Borrowed capital is available to the company on a short-term and/or medium-term and/or long-term basis, while equity is indefinite. While debt with one year or less maturity is considered to be short term; debt having maturity greater than one year is generally known as long term. Long-term debt is usually paid back in systematic amounts during the term of the debt with regularly scheduled interest payments. The share of equity in total capital is determined by the equity ratio, the corresponding proportion of borrowed capital with the debt ratio (Ross, Westerfield and Jaffe, 2013, p. 478).

The fundamental differences between debt and equity are listed by Ross, Westerfield and Jaffe, (2013, pp. 478–479) as follows:

1. Creditors typically do not have any authority in the administration and the right to vote.
2. Debt has an advantage of being fully tax deductible, but dividends do not.
3. Unpaid debt is the responsibility of the company, and if the payment is not made, the creditors can demand the assets of the company in accordance with the law. This activity may cause liquidation or restructuring, which are the two likely outcomes of bankruptcy. Therefore, issuing debt can cause financial distress. The same is not true for issuing equity.

A number of different objectives are used to determine the optimal capital structure. Claims for optimal capital structure results from the combination of cost and risk considerations of the company. Different ideas about the optimal capital structure arise because of the different individual objectives of the organization participants.

3.2 Theories of capital structure

Structure of capital has been explicated many times by different theories. The first model, which is revealed by Modigliani and Miller, is the basis of capital structure theories. Several theories have been developed after the Modigliani and Miller Irrelevance Theory. Some of these are concerned with the meaninglessness of capital structure, some with asymmetric information and others with psychological factors.

In this part of the study, the capital structure theories are taken into account.

3.2.1 Modigliani and Miller Irrelevance Theory

The irrelevance theorem for corporate finance is one of the most important models of financial management. For today it still serves as the basis of modern capital market theory. The irrelevance theorem goes back to the two economists Franco Modigliani and Merton H. Miller, who were also awarded the Nobel Prize in Economics for their work in 1990.

Modigliani and Miller (1958) assume a perfect capital market. The irrelevance theorem states that capital structure decisions have no effect on the market value of a company. This means that the proportion of a company's equity and borrowed capital is irrelevant to the asset position of the shareholders. The irrelevance theorem was theoretically proved by Modigliani and Miller with the help of the arbitration. Arbitrage is the possibility of making profits by taking advantage of price differences. The irrelevance theorem is based on very rigid conditions such as the absence of insolvency costs or finance-related taxes. This is based on strongly simplifying assumptions and therefore has little relevance in direct practical implementation. In practice, however, these assumptions are difficult to maintain. Nevertheless, the irrelevance theorem is used as a starting point for further investigations into capital structure decisions. It analyzes how the non-fulfillment of individual conditions, such as the occurrence of insolvency costs, impacts the capital structure decisions of companies.

The assumptions of the theory of Modigliani and Miller (1958, 1963) can be listed as follows (Copeland and Weston, 1988, p. 439):

- Capital markets do not create frictions.
- Everyone can borrow and lend at the risk-free rate (a uniform risk-free interest rate exists).
- There is no bankruptcy cost.
- There are only two types of claims that firms issue: risk-free debt and (risky) equity.
- It is assumed that risk class is same for all firms (they do not differ in terms of their business risk).
- The government imposes only corporate taxes (there are not any other taxes like wealth taxes on corporations or personal taxes).
- All cash flow streams last forever (there is no growth).
- All the information is available for both corporate insiders and outsiders (there is no information asymmetry).
- The objective of managers is maximizing shareholders' wealth (there are no agency costs).

There are two propositions of the Modigliani and Miller Irrelevance Theory. The first proposition of Modigliani and Miller accept that in a perfect capital market, the total value of a firm is the same as the market value of the total cash flows created by its assets (Berk and DeMarzo, 2011, p. 162). It claims that financial leverage which is the rate of debt financing, is irrelevant and the type of securities do not have any significant effect on the total value of a firm. Additionally, Proposition 1 also assumes that the cost of capital of the firm is constant, it does not change according to debt ratio (Myers, 2001, p. 84). As a result of using, debt financing takes the place of the higher cost of equity with lower costing debt, the cost of capital to stay unchanging, the cost of equity must grow with leverage. This linear relationship is referred to as Modigliani-Miller Proposition 2 (Pettengill and Lander, 2015, p. 111). It says that the advantage from the increase in usage of low-cost debt and a decrease in usage of high-cost equity is entirely offset by the increase in the risk level of equity. In other words, leverage has no effect on the cost of capital (Marinsek et al., 2015,

p. 73). Myers explain this proposition as "no magic in financial leverage" (Myers, 2001 p. 6).

3.2.2 Trade-Off Theory

After the publication of the Modigliani-Miller theorem, initial attempts have been made to explore the effects of the basic assumptions. The first significant contribution of this period comes from Modigliani and Miller themselves. Modigliani and Miller already recognized in their publication of 1958 that their model must be adapted to take account of the tax deductibility of borrowed capital and the first corrections were made in 1963, and the correct adjustment of the tax advantage of the debt financing is included in the model (Modigliani and Miller, 1963). In addition to taxation, there should be other factors that affect the capital structure, and in the following years, the insolvency risk of debt was started to be considered. In 1967, Baxter emphasized the importance of insolvency costs as part of a qualitative contribution. In his opinion, insolvency costs are the main opponents of the tax advantages. Due to the rising risk of insolvency, Baxter sees Modigliani and Miller's arbitrage mechanism suspended in situations of extreme indebtedness because investors are no longer willing to take excessive risk. The insolvency risk also develops nonlinearity. A slight debt increases the probability of insolvency, while a considerable reduction in the equity ratio will have a significant impact on the probability of insolvency (Baxter, 1967, pp. 395–403).

The Trade-Off Theory of capital structure states that a company determines its debt and equity level according to its cost and benefits. The theory basically involves offsetting the costs of debt against the benefits of debt. It primarily takes the necessary action, especially in reference to two concepts, cost of financial distress and agency costs. It says that financing with debt gives firms an advantage, which is the tax benefit of debt. There is a cost of financing with debt as well, which is the cost of financial distress including bankruptcy. So, a firm that wants to optimize its overall value should focus on the trade-off between debt and equity.

The Trade-Off Theory is based on the study of Kraus and Litzenberger (1973). Like Modigliani and Miller Irrelevance Theory, they also state that in complete and perfect capital markets, the market value of a firm is independent of its capital structure. Furthermore, they said that the taxation of corporate gains and the presence of bankruptcy penalties have an effect of leverage on the firm's market value. Kraus and Litzenberger introduced Static Trade-Off Theory which shows that the market value of a levered firm is equal to the unlevered market value, plus the corporate tax rate times the market value of the firm's debt, minus the complement of the corporate tax rate times the present value of bankruptcy costs. Lastly, they assume that if the firm's debt obligation is more than its earnings, at that time, the firm's market value is not certainly a concave function of its debt obligation (Kraus and Litzenberger, 1973, p. 918).

Market imperfections give rise to the emergence of bankruptcy costs, and the trade-off between bankruptcy costs and the tax subsidy enable an internal optimal capital structure. Haugen and Senbet (1978) show this view of optimal capital structure by discussing that bankruptcy costs that influence the capital structure decisions are unimportant if capital market prices are competitively determined by rational investors. If the opposite is the case and there is systematic irrationality and inefficient market environment, then investors want to buy or sell securities only at unfavorable terms (Haugen and Senbet, 1978). Scott (1976) and Kim (1978) also derived an optimal capital structure, taking into account corporate taxes and insolvency risks. According to their explanatory approach, the tax advantage of debt financing and the insolvency costs determine the choice of the capital structure. The classic Trade-Off Theory affirms an optimal, maximizing degree of debt. The maximum corporate value depending on the debt is assumed to be reached if the marginal tax advantages of debt financing just match the marginal expected insolvency costs. However, due to the fact that transaction costs exist in reality, it is not necessarily useful for a firm to maintain the optimal level of indebtedness. Rather, a rationally acting company will correct only deviations from the optimal capital structure in which the increase in the company value resulting from the recalibration of the capital structure exceeds the transaction costs associated with it. Finally, with the model of Myers (1984), a firm that acts according to the Trade-Off Theory puts a target debt value and then slowly moves towards this target to find optimum debt level, a viable explanatory model for the choice of capital structure appeared towards the middle of the 1980s. The target is specified by balancing debt tax shields against costs of bankruptcy which is illustrated in Figure 3.1. But, it is stated that if a firm uses Static Trade-Off Theory, then its leverage is determined by a single-period trade-off between tax benefit of debt and costs of bankruptcy. For diversified periods, the leverage ratio needs frequent rebalancing of debt and equity. Since the Static Trade-Off Theory only focuses on a single period and does not control the notion of target adjustment, Dynamic Trade-Off Theory should be used for multiple periods because keeping the leverage ratio constant all the time will be costly for the firm, even though it is optimal at that period (Bessler, Drobetz and Kazemieh, 2011, p. 19).

Figure 3.1: The Static Trade-Off Theory of capital structure

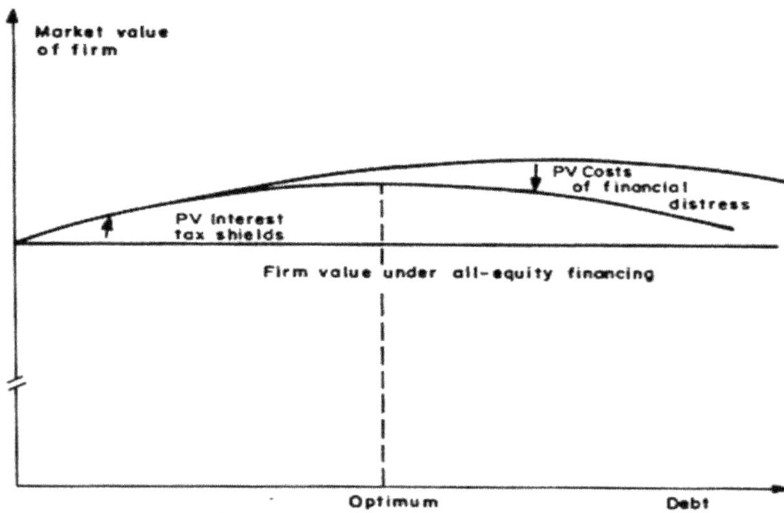

Source: Myers, 1984, p. 30.

3.2.3 Pecking Order Theory

The Pecking Order Theory concentrates on the information asymmetry between management and investors. Managers, of course, know more than investors about the real position of the company. This leads to managers acting as insiders in obtaining additional funds. The assumptions are based on the fact that management chooses the form of financing in the interests of the company and the existing shareholders. The asymmetry of information affects the selection between internal and external financing.

The preference of the chosen type of financing is also derived from the size and profitability of a company.

First, companies are financed from operating cash flow and, if further capital is needed, borrowed capital is preferred to equity. The issuance of new shares is considered to be the last option and only applied in cases where the debt-to-equity ratio has been exhausted. An equity investment sends negative signals to investors. The chosen date for the issuance of new shares is interpreted by new shareholders as a phase of an enterprise overvaluation. On the other hand, the acquisition of equity is not financially interesting. The asymmetry of information thus favors borrowing before the issue of equity capital. For managers as well as investors act rationally and try to anticipate the thoughts and consequences of the other party (Myers and Majluf, 1984).

The idea of Meyer that firms prefer internal to external finance because of adverse selection was refined by Shyam-Sunder and Myers in 1999, and a model was established as follows (Shyam-Sunder and Myers, 1999):

$$DEFt = DIVt + Xt + \Delta Wt + Rt - Ct \quad \text{(Eq. 1)}$$

Where;

Ct: operating cash flows, after interest and taxes at the end of period t
DIVt: dividend payments at the end of period t
Xt: capital expenditures at the end of period t
ΔWt: net increase in working capital at the end of period t
Rt: current portion of long-term debt at start period

This simplest form of the pecking order model indicates that if the internal cash flows are insufficient for the firms' future investments and dividend commitments, then the firm issues debt. Equity is the last resort and could be used only when financial distress is very heavy.

3.2.4 Agency Theory

Jensen and Meckling (1976) define agency relationship as: "*a contract under which one or more persons (the principal(s)) engage another person (the agent) to perform some service on their behalf which involves delegating some decision making authority to the agent.*" When both sides of this relationship try to maximize their own utility, it is assumed that the agent will not always act in the interests of the principal. Appropriate incentives and monitoring costs can help principal to limit this incorrect behavior of the agent (Jensen and Meckling, 1976).

In order to mitigate the conflicts of interests between the principal and the agent, two basic solutions are available. On the one hand, the principal can influence the agent (monitoring) by means of incentive and control mechanisms. On the other hand, the agent can, in various forms of voluntary self-commitment, underline his willingness to conduct interest-related behavior (bonding). Since, despite monitoring and bonding mechanisms, an optimal behavior of the agent cannot be achieved as expected, therefore, there remains a loss of welfare on the part of the principal, which the Agency Theory calls the residual loss. The sum of monitoring costs, bonding costs and residual loss generate the total agency costs of a principal-agent relationship. The insight of the study of Jensen and Meckling indicate that the financing decisions could justify and influence the principle-agent relationship. According to Jensen and Meckling, such relationships occur between managers (agents) and company-oriented equity investors (principals), as well as between equity owners (agents) and company-oriented third-party lenders (principals). Principals anticipate possible misbehavior of the agents and take into account the expected monitoring costs and the expected residual loss in the company assessment. Consequently, financing-related agency conflicts lead to a decline in corporate value. With this basic finding, Jensen and Meckling open a completely new perspective on the relationship between capital structure and corporate value.

The problem in the principal-agent relationship results from the fact that the agent does not strictly pursue the interests of the principal. The principal cannot be completely informed about the behavior of the agent. The information asymmetries represent the cause of behavioral risks which endanger the interests of the principal in the execution of the contract. The information asymmetries can refer to hidden information as well as to hidden intention and to hidden actions of the agent. The article by Jensen and Meckling discusses the interaction between the manager, the other equity providers and the borrower. The results of their study are relevant in that, apart from the agency conflict between the manager and the equity investor, there can also be such a conflict between equity providers and borrowers, and the possibility of agency cost reduction can be achieved by mixing the two types of capital. This is done by finding an optimal trade-off of these costs (Jensen and Meckling, 1976).

The conflict between debt holders and equity holders appear since the debt contract encourages equity holders to invest inappropriately. In other words, the debt contract makes it available that if an investment produces large returns, which is above the face value of the debt, then equity holders get most of the gain. But, if the investment does not succeed, because of inadequate liability, then debt holders carry the consequences. Hereby, equity holders may invest in very risky projects, without considering that risky projects may decrease the overall value. These kinds of investments follow a decrease in the value of the debt (Harris and Raviv, 1991).

Companies get advantage from indebtedness until the point on the increase of its value owed to the financed investments will be equal to the marginal costs created by the indebtedness. Consequently, the optimal quantity of indebtedness is the amount that makes the minimization of overall agency costs possible, which are the costs related to indebtedness and to appeal to external own funds. Grigore and Ştefan-Duicu (2013) emphasize that identifying the optimal capital structure does not mean just the arrangement of debts and equity, but also specifying the part of equity owned by managers and the part of equity owned by other shareholders. They represent agency costs, as shown graphically in Figure 3.2.

- Ase(E): agency cost depending on E, related to own external funds
- AD(E): agency cost also depending on E, related to debts.
- AT(E) = total agency costs, equal to Ase(E) + AD(E).
- E* is the level for which the total agency costs, noted AT(E*) are minimal.

ASe(E), when E is equal to null that means there is no external own fund, then the manager does not want to use external own funds. Additionally, any change in .the amount of the external own funds is equal to the change of value in the own funds owned by the manager; for this reason, there is no agency cost and any rise in E means there is an increase of the level of a manager's motivation. In the opposite case, when E is equal to hundred percent, the agency cost will be highest. By looking at AD(E), which represent the agency cost that follows as the consequence of indebtedness and arises since the manager encourages to transfer a share of the profit from the benefit of the creditors to itself. Eventually, this transfer increases the own fund value (Grigore and Ştefan-Duicu, 2013, p. 865).

Figure 3.2: Agency costs depending on funding sources

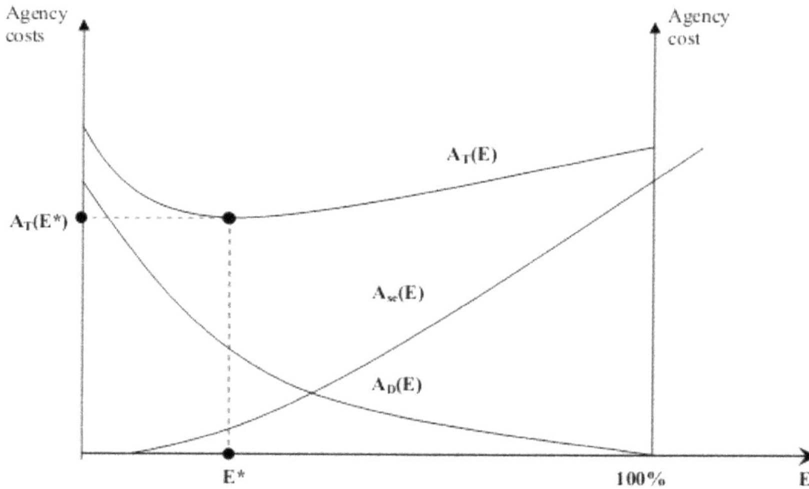

Source: Grigore and Ştefan-Duicu, 2013, p. 866.

3.3 Empirical research on the determination of capital structure

3.3.1 Determinants of firms capital structure

A key research subject of modern corporate finance is the choice of the optimal capital structure of companies. The main matter is whether and how financing decisions affect the cost of capital and the market value of a company. The choice of the optimal capital structure also has immense importance for financial management. The starting point is the question of whether the capital costs are reduced for a given capital volume by a change in the level of debt or an exchange of the financing instruments on the liabilities side, thereby increasing the market value of the company.

An early investigation is performed by Titman and Wessels (1988) who aimed to examine capital structure theories and the measures of short-term, long-term and convertible debt. The analysis was based on the large 469 US firms for the period 1974–1982. As explanatory variables expected future growth, non-debt tax shields, asset structure and industry classification, size, profitability and change in operating income were used. Of all these factors, only a negative correlation was found between firm size and short-term debt ratios.

Based on the dataset of 972 firms listed on the Shanghai Stock Exchange and Shenzhen Stock Exchange, Chen and Strange (2005) examine the determinants of the capital structure. As a dependent variable, they use total liabilities to total book value ratio and total liabilities to total liabilities plus the market value of common stock. On the other hand, as an explanatory variable, they use three different groups of variables. The first group includes seven variables that are used most commonly in the literature. The second group includes four ownership structure variables, and the third group involves eighteen industry dummy variables. The results of the Ordinary Least Squares analysis shows that profitability and ownership structure are negative; size, risk and the age of companies are positively related to capital structure. They couldn't find any relation between tax and debt ratio. In another study, Fattouh, Harris and Scaramozzino (2008) evaluate the determinants of capital structure of 6614 UK-listed companies by using conditional quantile regression analysis between the years 1988–1998, inclusive. The distinguishing feature of this study rests upon its prediction by exploiting more fully the distribution of leverage. The findings are supportive of a significant relationship between leverage and size that is calculated in two different way, the logarithm of total sales and total assets. They conclude that this significant relationship is positive for lower quantiles and it is negative for firms in the upper quantiles.

Another considerable research done on determinants of capital structure is the one conducted by Psillaki and Daskalakis (2009). In this research, they utilize a balanced panel data model to evaluate the capital structure of Greek, French, Italian and Portuguese Small and Medium-Sized Enterprises (SMEs). They study how asset structure, size, profitability, risk and growth affect capital structure of these different countries. The findings support that the determinants of the SMEs of Greek, French, Italian and Portuguese are similar. Where the link is found to be insignificant between growth and leverage, they found a positive significant relationship between size and leverage and a negative relationship between leverage and asset structure, profitability and risk for these four countries. Based on this reasoning, they conclude that firm-specific variables can explain the differences in capital structure choices of SMEs rather than the country-specific determinants.

Mazur (2007) analyzed which basic theory of capital structure, the pecking order or the traditional Static Trade-Off model explained the financing decisions of Polish companies better. Assets structure, profitability, growth opportunities, liquidity, firm size, product uniqueness, earnings volatility, non-debt tax shields, dividend policy and the effective tax rate are chosen as independent variables to determine its effect on capital structure with multiple regressions. The author suggests that Pecking Order Theory explains the financing choices of Polish firms. The analysis resulted in a positive relationship between profitability and leverage for highly profitable firms. On the other hand, there is not a significant relation between profitability, liquidity, assets structure, growth opportunities, size and uniqueness and effective tax rate or non-debt tax shields. That is the reason why the author concludes that the Trade-Off Theory is not applicable for the Polish firms.

Even though there are a wide variety of empirical studies that assume the determinants of optimal capital structure of large publicly-traded manufacturing firms; but there are not too many studies which explain the debt/equity choice of firms that are private, small or not operated in the manufacturing industry. In their study, Köksal and Orman (2015) take measures to check the Trade-Off and Pecking Order theories with a dataset that covers manufacturing, non-manufacturing, small, large, publicly traded and private firms in Turkey. Based on their argument, the Trade-Off Theory, which is suitable for large private firms in the non-manufacturing sector, explains the capital structure of all firm types better than the Pecking Order Theory, which is beneficial for small publicly traded manufacturing firms in unstable economic conditions.

Deesomsak, Paudyal and Pescetto (2004) analyze the financing decisions of 294 Thai, 669 Malaysian, 345 Singaporean and 219 Australian firms for the period 1993 to 2001. Tangibility, profitability, firm size, growth opportunity, non-debt tax shield, liquidity, earnings volatility and share price performance are chosen as firm-specific explanatory variables, and stock market's activity and level of interest rates as country-specific explanatory variables. They investigate that there is a positive relationship between firm size and leverage and a negative relationship between growth opportunities, non-debt tax shield, liquidity and share price performance and leverage.

Additionally, the importance of the determinants of capital structure change across countries in the Asia-Pacific region.

Another study that concludes the debt-to-equity ratio of firms grows with size and fixed assets, and becomes smaller with profitability, non-debt tax shields, growth opportunity and managerial shareholdings is that of Huang and Song (2006. The analysis utilizes book long-term debt ratio, book total debt ratio, book total liabilities ratio, market long-term debt ratio, market total debt ratio and market total liabilities ratio as the indicator of leverage on a dataset of 1200 Chinese-listed companies during the 1994–2003 period making up a total of 12000 firm-year observations. The findings of the study determine that state ownership or institutional ownership has no significant impact on the capital structure and Chinese firms tend to have much lower long-term debt as a result of preferring and having access to equity financing when they go public.

Bayrakdaroğlu, Ege and Yazıcı (2013) investigate the capital structure determinants of 242 Turkish companies using firm-level data for the period 2000–2009. They find that Turkish companies which follow a hierarchical company structure are not trying to achieve a special debt ratio. Like most of the other studies, profitability, tangibility of assets, size, growth opportunities, non-debt tax shields, inflation and taxes are chosen as explanatory variables. The authors argue that the Pecking Order Theory explain the capital structure of the Turkish companies better than Trade-Off Theory and that is why Turkish companies are using Pecking Order Theory for determining their debt behaviors. While empirical study resulted in a positive relationship between size, growth opportunities, tax and total debt ratio; it resulted in a negative relationship between profitability, fixed assets, inflation and debt ratio.

3.3.2 Determinants of banks' capital structure

This subsection of the book focuses on the empirical literature on non-financial firms to explain the capital structure of banks. Studies on the empirical analysis of the determinants of the bank capital structure usually take account of both internal and external factors of determination. Sharpe (1995 examines the determinants of capital structure of Australian trading banks over the period 1967–1988. He indicates that long-run capital ratios are negatively correlated with expected growth opportunities and positively correlated with expected retained profits. Conversely, he finds little support for the predictions of the bankruptcy cost and tax benefit theory of optimal capital structure. Vo (2017) comprehensively discusses whether capital structure determinants are different in emerging markets and find that the determinants of capital structure are different for long-term and short-term indicators for Vietnam banking market. He takes a large number of bank-specific variables such as asset growth, ratio of tangible assets, profit, firm size and liquidity into account while explaining capital structure. Vo found that the determinants of capital structure are different for long-term and short-term leverage. Jouida and Hallara (2015), who are studying this issue for the French banking market, came to a similar conclusion. They use panel data regression analysis on French banks between the periods of 2002–2012 and try to find the determinants of bank capital structure. Their results show that the bank characteristic determinants like size, profitability, growth, risk, collateral and dividends clarify a big amount of the variation of bank leverage, although the ability of explanation rate becomes lower while introducing Tier 1 Capital Ratio. In addition, the heterogeneity of the country and time level has a big explanatory power on the variation in the leverage ratios. While the research results of the above studies are based on data sets relating to banks of a specific country, cross-country studies also exist. For example, the work of Gropp and Heider (2009) examines the capital structure of large US and European banks during 1991–2004, taking into account bank-specific and macroeconomic factors influencing the overall regulation on capital. The authors document a significant positive correlation between the leverage and market-to-book ratio, profitability, size and collateral but they do not find a significant effect of deposit insurance on the capital structure. Sha'ban, Girardone and Sarkisyan (2016) investigate comparable factors for the European Economic Area's listed commercial banks. They add the global financial crisis and the euro sovereign debt crisis into their model and also examine moral hazard effects that come from the too-big-to-fail status and alternative types of risk. They show that profits, market-to-book ratios and dividends have a significant positive impact on the equity capital, while size is significantly negative. However, asset quality measured by nonperforming loans do not provide a significant explanation. They show that market risk significantly increases banks' equity capital, which proves the regulatory aspect that riskier banks are forced to hold higher equity. Nguyen and Kayani (2013) investigate the importance of firm-specific determinants as compared to macroeconomic factors on capital structure decision of banks for the 61 banks from 10 Asian countries (5 developed and 5 developing countries) from 2000 to 2012. They show that the capital structures of banks rely upon the economic growth level of the countries. They also conclude that collateral has a significant effect only on the capital mix of banks of developed countries, but profit is significant just or the banks in developing countries. Tax and GDP are the macroeconomic variables which have an effect on the banks' capital structure. Papagianni (2013) also concludes that the accepted determinants of capital structure have an explanatory power on leverage. Their sample includes listed commercial banks of the European Union of 15 countries between the period 2007 and 2012. They determine that size, profitability, the ratio liquid assets to deposits and short-term funding and the ratio of net loans to total assets and tangibility have a significant effect on banks' capital structure. On the other hand, they find that inflation has an effect on leverage but GDP growth rate does not. Octavia and Brown (2010) examined whether the accepted determinants of capital structure are significant factors in determining the level of bank capital in developing countries. They work with a sample of listed commercial banks from 10 developing countries and find that size, profitability, market-to-book ratio, collateral, dividend, asset risk, GDP, stock market risk have explanatory power in determining book leverage but have insignificant explanatory power on market leverage.

4 Research design

4.1 Procyclicality of leverage

4.1.1 Data and sample selection

The data used in the empirical part of this book covers the period between January 2005 and December 2014. The details of the dependent, independent and control variables of the models held on the databases of the Banking Regulation and Supervision Agency (BDDK) and Central Bank of Turkey. The sample comprises all of the commercial, participation, development and investment banks and banking sector information during the ten years (one hundred and twenty months) observation period.

The bank sample is provided in Table 4.1 below. It includes the number of all banks at the end of the last month of the year that were used in this study.

Table 4.1: The Number of Banks at the End of the Last Month of the Year

	Banking Sector	Commercial Banks	Participation Banks	Development-Investment Banks
2014	49	32	4	13
2013	49	32	4	13
2012	49	32	4	13
2011	48	31	4	13
2010	49	32	4	13
2009	49	32	4	13
2008	49	32	4	13
2007	50	33	4	13
2006	50	33	4	13
2005	51	34	4	13

Analyses were performed with a total of 360 bank-year observations. All commercial, participation and development and investment banks are included, and for performing the analysis software package STATA 13 is used.

As can be seen, Turkish financial system is dominated by commercial banks. More than sixty percent of all banks operating in Turkey are commercial. They reached a total asset of 2,122,513.292 million Turkish Lira with 11157 domestic branches and 194396 employees in October 2015. On the other hand, development and investment banks have 105,482.262 million Turkish Lira of total asset, 40 domestic branches and 5374 employees in the same time period. The minimum share in the banking sector belongs to participation banks. The four banks operating in the participation banking sector achieved total assets of 110 billion Turkish Lira at the end of March 2015. With the contribution of Ziraat Participation Bank, the number of participation banks rose to five in the banking sector. Now the share of participant banks increased to 5 percent from 2 percent. They have 119,719.468 million Turkish Lira worth of assets, a total of 990 branches and about 17 thousand people are employed by the end of 2014.

4.1.2 The variables

There is a detailed explanation of the variables in Table 4.2. It includes the entire dependent, independent and control variables, their abbreviations and definitions. Eight different leverage ratios are used as dependent variables and therefore, eight different models are established with different dependent variables and the same explanatory variable and control variables. There is one explanatory variable as asset growth. For control variables, firm size and inflation are chosen.

Table 4.2: Variables, Abbreviations and Definitions

Variable	Abbreviation	Definition
Leverage-1	leverage1	The ratio of total assets to total equity
Leverage-2	leverage2	The ratio of total debt to total equity
Leverage-3	leverage3	The ratio of the sum of the total debt and off balance sheet liabilities to total equity
Leverage-4	leverage4	The ratio of the difference between Tier 1 capital and regulatory deductions to the ratio of the sum of the total assets and off balance sheet liabilities
Leverage-5	leverage5	The ratio of the difference between Tier 1 capital and regulatory deductions to the ratio of the sum of the total debt and off balance sheet liabilities
Leverage-6	leverage6	The ratio of Tier 1 capital to adjusted assets
Leverage-7	leverage7	One minus the ratio of total equity to total assets
Leverage-8	leverage8	The ratio of the value at risk to total equity
Total Assets	asset	Total book value of intangible, tangible and other fixed assets.

Variable	Abbreviation	Definition
Asset Growth	assetgrowth	The ratio of the difference between the current month value of asset and the prior month value of asset to the value of prior month asset
Total Equity	equity	Total book value of equity
Total Debt		Total book value of short-term and long-term debt
Adjusted Assets	adjst	Book value of total assets excluding goodwill and intangible assets
Off Balance Sheet Liabilities	offblnc	The liabilities that are not included on balance sheet.
Tier 1 Capital	capital	Core capital
Regulatory Deduction	deduction	Deductions from core capital
Value at Risk	VaR	A measure of market risk
Firm Size	logsize	Natural log of total assets
Inflation	CPI	The rate of consumer price index inflation

4.1.2.1 The dependent variables

One of the aims of this book is determining the leverage behavior of Turkish banks according to the change in asset values. In accordance with this purpose, different leverage ratios are used as dependent variable in different models. In literature, there are different types of calculations for leverage ratios. There are the traditional and commonly used leverage calculations and also the unused and only recently began to be used ones. Table 4.3 includes the all dependent variables and their formulations.

Table 4.3: Leverage Ratios

Leverage-1	Total Assets/Total Equity
Leverage-2	Total Debt/Total Equity
Leverage-3	(Total Debt + Off Balance Sheet Liabilities) / Total Equity
Leverage-4	(Tier 1 Capital-Regulatory Deductions) / (Total Assets + Off Balance Sheet Liabilities)
Leverage-5	(Tier 1 Capital-Regulatory Deductions) / (Total Debt + Off Balance Sheet Liabilities)
Leverage-6	Tier 1 Capital/Adjusted Assets
Leverage-7	1- (Total Equity/Total Assets)
Leverage-8	VaR / Total Equity

Notes: Leverage 3–4 and 5 are taken from the study of Binici and Köksal (2012)

4.1.2.2 *The explanatory variable*

In this study, asset growth acts as a proxy of leverage. Change in asset value is considered as an indicator of the economic situation. It is accepted that when the asset value of a bank gets larger, then there is an economic boom and when the asset value of a bank gets smaller, there is an economic bust. In parallel with the increase in asset prices, banks take more short-term debt to achieve a constant target leverage ratio. With this, short-term debts banks purchase longer-term securities that bring higher returns than the debt they borrowed from others. When all banks demand more asset in the market, then this makes the asset prices to increase and make the economic conditions relatively better. In the opposite situation, when the asset prices decreases, which is referred as deflation, then the banks sell their assets and repay their debt to achieve the constant target leverage ratio, and this makes the economy worse (Çalışkan, 2011).

In line with most empirical studies, Beccalli, Boitani and Giuliantonio (2015), Laux and Rauter (2016), Binici and Köksal (2012), Adrian and Schin (2010), Baglioni, Beccalli, Boitani and Monticini (2012), Zadeh, Barth and Landsman (2017), Broden and Olovsson (2011) and Çalışkan (2011), asset growth is chosen as the only proxy, which is the growth rate of the value of total assets of banks. It is the ratio of the difference between the current month and the prior month value of the asset to the value of prior month asset. This explanatory variable helps us to understand the cyclical behavior of banks leverage.

4.1.2.3 *The control variables*

Several control variables have been chosen to be included in the models for eliminating the likely impact of various bank and industry-specific factors on leverage and understand exactly whether there is a relationship between asset growth and leverage. Natural log of total assets and Consumer Price Index have been taken as control variables.

Size is one of the most important determinants of capital structure. There are different opinions about the impact of size on leverage. According to Titman and Wessels (1988), Rajan and Zingales (1995), Heshmati (2001), Fama and French (2002), Bevan and Danbolt (2004) and Khalid (2011), large and high profitability firms tend to borrow less, which is inconsistent with the Trade-Off Ttheory that argues that higher profitability firms should borrow more to use tax benefit of debt. They claim that large firms are more transparent compared to the smaller ones, and therefore they issue more equity relative to debt and this causes a negative relation based on the Pecking Order Theory of the capital structure. On the other side, many studies support Agency Theory and trade-off that claims larger firms are more diversified and have less bankruptcy risk, and found a positive relationship between two variables (Jensen, 1986; Warner, 1977; Ang et al., 1982; Chittenden et al., 1996; Booth et al., 2001; Hovakimian, Opler and Titman, 2001; Korajczyk and Levy, 2003; Hovakimian et al., 2004; Flannery and Rangan, 2006).

Inflation has always been a major problem for Turkey. The banking sector problems, which were based on unsustainable domestic debt dynamics and the structural problems, could not be solved for a long time because of high and unstable inflation. For a long time, banks in Turkey did not use inflation accounting (that means the banks didn't correct their balance sheet according to the impact of inflation) and they ignored the inflationary effect. These conditions make debt financing more favorable than equity financing (BRSA, 2010). There are several ways to link inflation and leverage. Inflation leads firms to use more of debt since the real cost of debt declines when there is high inflation (Kim and Wu, 1988). According to the Trade-Off Theory, this means a positive connection between inflation and leverage. In her study, Işık (2004) states that a high rate of inflation increases positive expectations regarding future capital gains, reduce borrowing costs and encourage more borrowing. As a consequence, the high rate of inflation could cause a leverage growth. In Turkey, Çalışkan (2011) tried to test whether the inflation had a big impact on leverage as it did in the 1990s before the regulations. For the period 2002–2009, he couldn't find any significant relationship between leverage and inflation.

In line with the most empirical studies and above provided reasoning, this study employs size and inflation as control variables.

4.1.3 Descriptive statistics

The descriptive statistics of all variables included in the empirical part of this study for the ten year period between 2005 and 2014 are provided in this subsection. Firstly, the results based on the summary statistics of the dependent variables will be evaluated, followed by those of the independent and control variables.

Based on the findings provided in Table 4.4 below, it is clear that the mean of 8 leverage ratios differs among themselves for each banking group. The first leverage ratio which is the ratio of total assets to total equity is highest for participant banks that officially began its activities in 2001 in Turkey. The mean ratio of Leverage 1 for Commercial Banks is on average 8.58 with a standard deviation 0.61, and it is very close to the rate of Participant Banks. The wide range of distribution that occurs due to the minimum and maximum values of 6.85 and 9.95 shows that there isn't too much differences between the years as can be seen by the small standard deviation. This ratio is very low for the Development and Investment Banks with a mean value 2.52. It is the same for the second Leverage ratio. Evaluation of Leverage 2 represents the ratio of total debt to total equity shows that the mean and standard deviation of Leverage ratio 2 for Commercial Banks is 7.58 and 0.61, respectively. It is approximately the same for Participant Banks with a mean value of 8 and with a standard deviation of 1.30. An evaluation of the maximum and minimum values of 5.91 and 10.73 reveal the wide range of distribution belonging to the variable Leverage 2 meaning that not a big amount of variability exists in terms of years.

Table 4.4: Descriptive Statistics of Leverage Ratios

	Banking Sector				Commercial Banks				Participation Banks				Development-Investment Banks			
	Mean	Std. Dev.	Min.	Max.	Mean	Std. Dev.	Min.	Max.	Mean	Std. Dev.	Min.	Max.	Mean	Std. Dev.	Min.	Max.
Leverage-1	7.916	0.564	6.378	9.189	8.581	0.614	6.845	9.951	9.007	1.296	6.911	11.733	2.522	0.612	1.921	3.986
Leverage-2	6.916	0.564	5.378	8.189	7.581	0.614	5.845	8.951	8.007	1.296	5.911	10.733	1.522	0.612	0.921	2.986
Leverage-3	14.186	3.030	8.723	21.104	16.087	3.381	9.654	23.695	18.133	6.139	12.816	35.363	3.354	1.294	1.795	5.902
Leverage-4	0.062	0.009	0.041	0.082	0.055	0.008	0.037	0.073	0.054	0.012	0.026	0.069	0.245	0.063	0.144	0.340
Leverage-5	0.067	0.011	0.043	0.091	0.058	0.009	0.038	0.080	0.057	0.013	0.027	0.074	0.335	0.112	0.168	0.530
Leverage-6	0.124	0.007	0.109	0.145	0.114	0.005	0.101	0.133	0.112	0.016	0.086	0.146	0.418	0.082	0.251	0.518
Leverage-7	0.873	0.009	0.843	0.891	0.883	0.009	0.854	0.899	0.887	0.016	0.855	0.915	0.584	0.081	0.479	0.749
Leverage-8	0.244	0.065	0.123	0.415	0.269	0.075	0.121	0.452	0.075	0.046	0.019	0.228	0.106	0.027	0.047	0.187

Summary statistics based on Leverage 3 ratio displays that the mean values of the ratio of the sum of the total debt and off-balance sheet liabilities to total equity for commercial banks is 16.09, for participation banks is 18.13 and for development and investment Banks is 3.35, respectively. The maximum value of the Leverage 3 ratio reach 23.7 for commercial banks and 35.36 for participation banks and there are huge differences between maximum and minimum values of Leverage 3 ratios for these two banking group which show that off-balance sheet liabilities have a big effect on the leverage ratio as can also be seen by the large standard deviations of 3.38 and 6.14.

Focusing on the ratio of the difference between Tier 1 capital and regulatory deductions to the ratio of the sum of the total assets and off-balance sheet liabilities provided by Leverage 4 hold an average of 0.055 for commercial banks, 0.054 for participant banks and 0.245 for development and investment banks. The variation of Leverage 4 ratio is very small for each banking group. An evaluation of the minimum and maximum values of 0.037–0.073, 0.026–0.069, 0.144–0.340 demonstrate a narrow range of distribution belonging to the variable Leverage 4, which means not a considerable amount of variability exists in terms of Tier 1 capital and regulatory deductions.

Leverage 5, which is the ratio of the difference between Tier 1 capital and regulatory deductions to the ratio of the sum of the total debt and off-balance sheet liabilities and include all contingencies, letters of guarantee, bankers acceptance, letters of credit, endorsements and commitments, hold an average value of 0.058 for commercial banks, 0.057 for participant banks and 0.34 for development and investment banks. The small standard deviations of 0.009, 0.01 and 0.11 for these bank groups clearly present the variations in the leverage ratios of the sample banks. The difference between maximum and minimum values for the three bank groups is not huge.

The ratio of Tier 1 capital to adjusted assets provided by Leverage 6 reveals that the mean of commercial, participant and development and investment banks are 0.11, 0.11 and 0.42. The standard deviations of 0.005, 0.016 and 0.082 evidence that percentage of Leverage 6 ratio varies in a smaller extent across banks and time. The wide range of distribution that occurs due to the minimum and maximum values of 0.25–0.52 belong to the development and investment banks. Leverage 7, which is used by Gropp and Heider (2009 as a leverage ratio for financial institutions because of the claim that the standard calculations of leverage are not suitable for financial institutions while they do not take both debt and non-debt liabilities of banks such as deposits into consideration during determining leverage ratio, is calculated by one minus the ratio of total equity to total assets. The mean values of Leverage 7 are 0.88 for commercial banks, 0.88 for participant banks and 0.58 for development and investment banks, respectively. The standard deviation values for Leverage 7 are 0.008, 0.016 and 0.081 consecutively for commercial, participant and development and investment banks during the observation period. There is not a huge difference between the minimum and maximum values of Leverage 7 for three groups of banks. Leverage 8 includes more comprehensive and quantitative assessment risk concentrations that is the ratio of the value-at-risk to total equity. The mean values of Leverage 8 for commercial, participant and development and investment banks are 0.269 and 0.075 and 0.106, respectively.

Table 4.5: Descriptive Statistics of Explanatory Variables and Control Variables

	Banking Sector				Commercial Banks				Participation Banks				Development-Investment Banks			
	Mean	Std. Dev.	Min.	Max.	Mean	Std. Dev.	Min.	Max.	Mean	Std. Dev.	Min.	Max.	Mean	Std. Dev.	Min.	Max.
Asset Growth	0.016	0.019	-0.029	0.076	0.015	0.020	-0.028	0.075	0.023	0.023	-0.026	0.124	0.017	0.023	-0.043	0.092
Asset Size	5.389	0.228	5.489	6.299	5.886	0.223	5.463	6.257	4.502	0.346	3.844	5.018	4.452	0.260	4.041	4.927
CPI	174.47	39.31	114.49	248.82	174.478	39.313	114.49	248.82	174.48	39.313	114.49	248.82	174.478	39.31	114.49	248.82

Table 4.5 above displays the yearly statistics of selected explanatory and control variables, asset growth, asset size and inflation. The mean values for asset growth are 0.015, 0.023 and 0.018 for three groups of banks with standard deviations of 0.020, 0.023 and 0.023 during the observation period. The minimum and maximum values demonstrate a wide range of distribution that stand for a considerable amount of variability which exists in terms of asset growth. The mean value of Consumer Price Index is 174.478 Index Points for the observation period.

Figure 4.1: Growth of assets and leverage

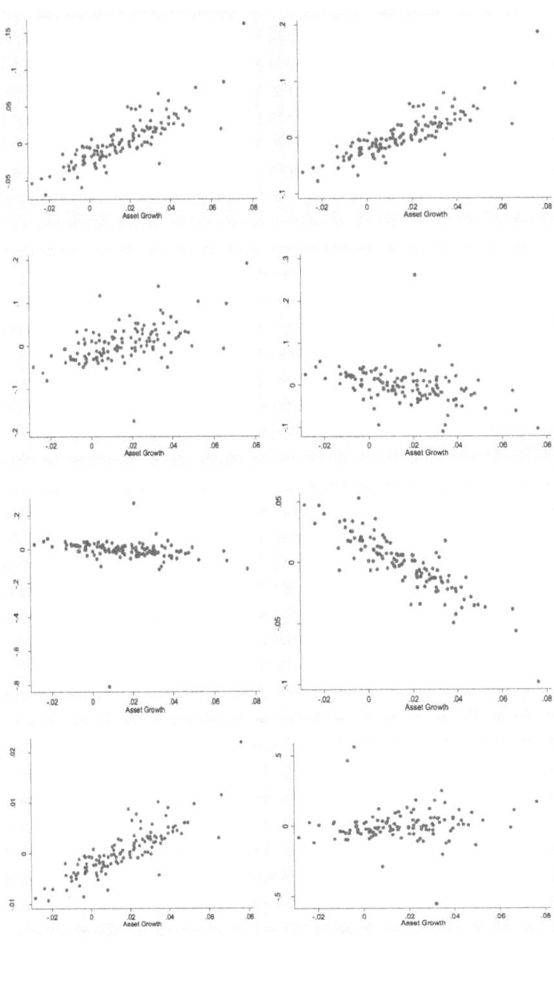

As can be seen from the Figure 4.1, there is a relation between asset growth and leverage growth. The direction of the association of Leverage 1 ratio and asset growth is very strong and positive, which means the values of Leverage 1 ratio tend to increase as the values of the asset increase. This situation is similar to the second leverage ratio which is going in the same direction with asset growth. On the other hand, the correlation between the Leverage 3 ratio and asset growth is positive, but this relation is not as strong as Leverage 1 and 2 ratios. The situation is somewhat different for Leverage 4 ratio. The correlation between Leverage 4 and asset growth is negative which causes an inverse relationship. The high values of asset growth are associated with low values of the Leverage 4 ratios. Similar to Leverage 4 ratio, there is a negative association between Leverage 5 and asset growth. The values of Leverage 5 tend to decrease as the values of the asset increase, but this relation is not too strong. As it is easily understood from the figure, the relationship between Leverage 7 and asset growth is positive because both variables move in tandem. The correlation between Leverage 8 ratio and asset growth is positive too, although this relation is not so powerful.

4.1.4 Empirical research model

Eight separate models are tested to determine the impact of asset growth on leverage which obtained from different calculations. With these models, the cyclical behavior of leverage is researched. The independent variable and control variables are the same for each model. The differences arise just due to the dependent variables. The findings are evaluated on the basis of random effect or fixed effect panel data analysis, which is selected according to the Hausman test results. Additionally, all models are also estimated using dummies, which make the random effect model a must.

Panel dates have both a time-series and a cross-sectional dimension for the same economic units (individuals, companies, countries) that are being observed over several time periods. The number of individuals, companies, countries (i = 1, ..., N) are usually much greater than the time dimension (t = 1, ..., T). The econometric model that takes into account the panel character of the data are referred to as panel data model.

In econometric modeling, it is assumed that the data can be pooled in a certain way. The simplest case of a linear panel data model is given by (Reyna, 2007, p. 10)

$$Yit = \alpha i + \beta 1Xit + \varepsilon i \qquad \textbf{(Eq. 2)}$$

Where:

- αi (i=1....n) is the intercept for each entity
- Yit is the dependent variable where i = entity and t = time
- Xit represents the independent variable
- $\beta 1$ is the coefficient (slope) for Xit
- εi is the error term

Advantages of Panel data can be listed as follows (Hsiao, 2006, pp. 3–8):

- In contrast to cross-sectional data, in panel data analysis there is more correct inference of model parameters.
- Panel data involves greater capacity for getting the complication of human attitude than a single cross-section or time-series data.
- Panel data make computation and statistical inference simpler.

There are two basic models for the analysis of panel data, the fixed effect model and the random effect model. In Table 4.6, Park (2011) compared the fixed and random effect models. He states that the only difference between fixed and random effect model arises from dummy variables. In a fixed effect model, a parameter approximate calculation of a dummy variable is included in the intercept and in the error component in a random effect model. Both models keep the slopes the same across groups or time periods.

Table 4.6: Fixed Effect and Random Effect Models

	Fixed Effect Model	Random Effect Model
Functional form	$Yit = (\alpha i + \varepsilon i) + \beta 1Xit + vi$	$Yit = \alpha i + \beta 1Xit + (\varepsilon i + vi)$
Assumption	-	Individual effects are not correlated with regressors
Intercepts	Varying across group and/or time	Constant
Error variances	Constant	Randomly distributed across group and/or time
Slopes	Constant	Constant
Estimation	LSDV, within effect estimation	GLS, FGLS (EGLS)
Hypothesis test	F test	Breusch-Pagan LM test

Source: Park, 2011, p. 8.

In random effect panel data analysis, the variation across entities is assumed to be random and uncorrelated with the predictor or independent variables. An advantage of random effect is that the time-invariant variables like gender can be included in the model contrary to the fixed effects model in which invariant variables are absorbed by the intercept. Random effect accepts that the error term of entities does not interact with the error term of predictors which pave the way for time-invariant variables to be explanatory variables. In random effect model, the individual characteristics should be specified and this situation can affect the predictor variables. In this case, due to the absence of some variables, there will be omitted variable bias in the model. Random effect model makes a general statement by inferring from the sample used in the model (Reyna, 2007).

4.1.4.1 *First model*

The first leverage ratio which widely used in financial literature is the value obtained from the relation between total assets and total equity. In their study, Adrian and Shin (2010), Çalışkan (2011), Broden and Olovsson (2011), Kalemli-Özcan, Sorensen and Yeşiltaş (2011) defined leverage as the ratio of total assets to total equity. This leverage ratio shows the amount of assets a bank holds relative to its equity and it determines how a bank manages its debt. The growth rate of this leverage ratio is taken as first dependent variable and it is tested whether there is an increasing (decreasing) trend in the leverage ratio of Turkish banks when there is an expansion (contraction) in their balance sheet.

The first-panel data estimation model, which evaluates the relationship between leverage-1 growth and the asset growth, can be demonstrated as in Equation 3 below:

$$Leverage\text{-}1\ Growthi,t = \beta 0 + \beta 1\ Assetgrowthi,t + \beta 2\ Sizei,t + \beta 3\ CPIi,t + \varepsilon i,t \quad \textbf{(Eq. 3)}$$

where;

Leverage-1 growth: the growth rate of leverage-1 ratio of banking group i in period t (periods are determined as monthly)

Asset growth: the growth rate of the value of total assets of banking group i in period t (periods are determined as monthly)

Size: natural log of total assets of banking group i in period t (the size of balance sheet)

CPI: the rate of consumer price index inflation in period t

$\varepsilon i,t$: error term in year t for banking group i

i: number of bank groups

t: time

The null and alternative hypotheses are the same for all eight models and they are established as follows. The results are evaluated according to these hypotheses. Null hypothesis says that the change in asset growth does not have any effect on leverage ratio and alternative hypothesis states that the asset growth has a significant influence on bank leverage.

H0: The independent variables have no explanatory power on bank leverage ($\beta i = 0$)

H1: The independent variables have significant explanatory power on bank leverage ($\beta i \neq 0$)

4.1.4.2 Second model

In the second model, debt-to-equity ratio is chosen as leverage in line with the studies of Ronald, Merle and Edgar (1996), Booth, Aivazian, Demirguç-Kunt and Maksimovic (2001). This leverage ratio has been used consistently in previous researches on capital structure decisions.

The second model is specified as in Equation 4 below:

$$Leverage\text{-}2\ Growth_{i,t} = \beta 0 + \beta 1\ Assetgrowth_{i,t} + \beta 2\ Size_{i,t} + \beta 3\ CPI_{i,t} + \varepsilon_{i,t} \qquad \text{(Eq. 4)}$$

where;

Leverage-2 Growth: the growth rate of leverage-2 ratio of banking group i in period t (period is determined as monthly) and all the other variables are defined and denoted as before.

4.1.4.3 Third model

In their studies, Brunnermeier (2009), Adrian and Shin (2010 and the Basel Committee on Banking Supervision Consultative Document have given clear reasons that banks caused the 2008 financial crises by providing a growing amount of their long-term liabilities with short-term liabilities through using the off-balance sheet items which composed of committed credits, guarantees and liquidity facilities. With having strong risk-based capital ratios, banks impose excessive off-balance sheet leverage on the banking system, and when faced with a crisis, the market pushes the banking sector to decrease its leverage which increases the strength of downward trend of asset prices. The combinations of all these events make the bad situation worse with the reduction in bank capital and scarcity of credit availability (Basel, 2013). Therefore, it is important to add off-balance sheet liabilities into the model and see the effect of this leverage ratio on balance sheet size.

The third model is specified as in Equation 5 below:

$$Leverage\text{-}3\ Growth_{i,t} = \beta 0 + \beta 1\ Assetgrowth_{i,t} + \beta 2\ Size_{i,t} + \beta 3\ CPI_{i,t} + \varepsilon_{i,t} \qquad \text{(Eq. 5)}$$

where;

Leverage-3 Growth: the growth rate of leverage-3 ratio of banking group i in period t (period is determined as monthly) and all the other variables are defined and denoted as before.

4.1.4.4 Fourth and fifth models

The fourth and fifth model also emphasizes the effect of balance sheet size on leverage ratio; however, it focuses specifically on Tier 1 Capital, regulatory deductions and off-balance sheet liabilities which are used as alternative leverage ratios in the study of Binici and Köksal (2012). The regulatory authorities use these leverage ratios as risk indicator in the banking system, or they are used as an indicator in the context of determined policies towards reducing the macro-financial risks. Contrary to the other leverage ratios, increase in Leverage-4 and Leverage-5 ratios stand for a reduction of debt (Binici and Köksal, 2012). Therefore, the fourth and fifth models that include all contingencies, letters of guarantee, bankers' acceptance, letters of credit, endorsements and commitments would produce coefficient estimates that are in the same magnitude but in opposite signs in comparison to other leverage ratios. The only difference between Leverage-4 and Leverage-5 ratios is the denominator values, one is calculated based on asset value and the other ratio is calculated based on debt value. Consistently, the models are estimated as in Equation 6 and Equation 7 below:

$$\textit{Leverage-4 Growthi,t} = \beta 0 + \beta 1\ \textit{Assetgrowthi,t} + \beta 2\ \textit{Sizei,t} + \beta 3\ \textit{CPIi,t} + \varepsilon \textit{i,t} \qquad \textbf{(Eq. 6)}$$

where;

Leverage-4 Growth: the growth rate of leverage-4 ratio of banking group i in period t (period is determined as monthly) and all the other variables are defined and denoted as before.

$$\textit{Leverage-5 Growthi,t} = \beta 0 + \beta 1\ \textit{Assetgrowthi,t} + \beta 2\ \textit{Sizei,t} + \beta 3\ \textit{CPIi,t} + \varepsilon \textit{i,t} \qquad \textbf{(Eq. 7)}$$

where;

Leverage-5 Growth: the growth rate of leverage-5 ratio of banking group i in period t (period is determined as monthly) and all the other variables are defined and denoted as before.

4.1.4.5 Sixth model

D'Hulster (2009) describes the leverage ratio as the ratio of Tier 1 capital to total adjusted assets. Tier 1 capital is obtained by deducting some intangible assets such as goodwill, software expenses and deferred tax assets from capital and reserves, and the adjusted assets are the remaining assets when we remove these intangible assets from total assets. In her study, D'Hulster (2009) defines the benefits of this leverage ratio as being countercyclical, simple and containing less regulatory arbitrage. While this leverage ratio offers these benefits, it is also subject to several weaknesses that should be taken into account. These weaknesses are, it may lead banks to taking wrong decisions since it does not distinguish different types of bank assets by their riskiness and it is limited to only balance sheet leverage, and does not include off-balance sheet items (D'Hulster, 2009). Accordingly, the sixth model focusing on Tier 1 capital and adjusted assets is constructed as in Equation 8 below:

$$\textit{Leverage-6 Growthi,t} = \beta 0 + \beta 1\ \textit{Assetgrowthi,t} + \beta 2\ \textit{Sizei,t} + \beta 3\ \textit{CPIi,t} + \varepsilon i,t \qquad \textbf{(Eq. 8)}$$

where;

Leverage-6 Growth: the growth rate of leverage-6 ratio of banking group i in period t (period is determined as monthly) and all the other variables are defined and denoted as before.

4.1.4.6 Seventh model

Gropp and Heider (2009 suggest that standard calculations of leverage are not suitable for financial institutions while they do not take both debt and non-debt liabilities of banks such as deposits into consideration while determining the leverage ratio. In their studies, by using leverage as one minus the ratio of total equity over total assets, they describe the decomposition of leverage (Gropp and Heider, 2010). Kalemli-Ozcan, Sorensen and Yesiltas (2011) have used this ratio as a benchmark measure to compare financial and nonfinancial firms leverage ratios. In seventh model this leverage ratio is used as a dependent variable which is constructed as in Equation 9 below:

$$\textit{Leverage-7 Growthi,t} = \beta 0 + \beta 1\ \textit{Assetgrowthi,t} + \beta 2\ \textit{Sizei,t} + \beta 3\ \textit{CPIi,t} + \varepsilon i,t \qquad \textbf{(Eq. 9)}$$

where;

Leverage-7 Growth: the growth rate of leverage-7 ratio of banking group i in period t (period is determined as monthly) and all the other variables are defined and denoted as before.

4.1.4.7 *Eighth model*

According to The President's Working Group on Financial Markets (1999), leverage ratio should include more comprehensive and quantitative assessment risk concentrations. They recommend banks to compare their value-at-risk ("VaR") numbers to the total amount of equities. In his study, Breuer (2000) defined leverage as "*a link between the risk of an asset position and the corresponding risk of an equity stake*". He mentioned that risk of the equity has two components which are the market risk of the asset and the leverage ratio with which this risk is translated to the equity position. He defined Value-at-Risk to total equity ratio not as a leverage ratio but as a measure of risk that measures whether there is sufficient equity to cover potential losses on the asset portfolio or not. In the eighth model, VaR to equity ratios are used for measuring banks leverages.

$$Leverage\text{-}8\ Growthi,t = \beta 0 + \beta 1\ Assetgrowthi,t + \beta 2\ Sizei,t + \beta 3\ CPIi,t + \varepsilon i,t \qquad \textbf{(Eq. 10)}$$

where;

Leverage-8 Growth: the growth rate of leverage-8 ratio of banking group i in period t (period is determined as monthly) and all the other variables are defined and denoted as before.

4.1.5 Data analysis and results

Table 4.7 presents the results of eight different models providing yearly evidence on the relationship between the leverage, asset growth and associated control variables. There is statistical validity for all of the yearly regressions means the p value of all the models are significant at $p<0.01$. Also, the goodness of fit measure indicated by adjusted R squared and Hausman test results are demonstrated in Table 4.7. It is also stated which model (fixed effect model or random effect model) is selected.

Table 4.7: The Relationship between Leverage Growth and Asset Growth

	Leverage-1	Leverage-2	Leverage-3	Leverage-4	Leverage-5	Leverage-6	Leverage-7	Leverage-8
Asset Growth	.961***	1.309***	.946***	-.670***	-.670***	-.833***	.351***	1.920***
	(.053)	(.069)	(.215)	(.140)	(.141)	(.049)	(.024)	(.539)
Size	.0033*	.003*	.002	-.003	-.018	-.059***	.009	-.007
	(.001)	(.002)	(.007)	(.005)	(.049)	(.017)	(.008)	(.018)
CPI	.001**	.001***	-.001	.000	.000	.000**	-.000	.000
	(.000)	(.000)	(.000)	(.000)	(.000)	(.000)	(.000)	(.000)
Constant	-.045***	-.056***	-.015	.021	.076	.251***	-.046	.000
	(.009)	(.011)	(.035)	(.023)	(.182)	(.063)	(.031)	(.088)
N	360	360	360	360	360	360	360	360
R-squared	0.481	0.508	0.052	0.061	0.045	0.083	0.222	0.036
Prob>chi2 (Hausman Test)	0.114	0.276	0.467	0.066	0.009	0.048	0.000	0.288
Fixed Effect	No	No	No	No	Yes	Yes	Yes	No

(Leverage-1: Total Assets / Total Equity, Leverage-2: Total Debt / Total Equity, Leverage-3: (Total Debt +Off Balance Sheet Liabilities) / Total Equity, Leverage-4: (Tier 1 Capital-Regulatory Deductions) / (Total Assets +Off Balance Sheet Liabilities), Leverage-5: (Tier 1 Capital-Regulatory Deductions) / (Total Debt + Off Balance Sheet Liabilities), Leverage-6: Tier 1 Capital / Adjusted Assets, Leverage-7: 1- (Total Equity / Total Assets), Leverage-8: VaR / Total Equity)

Notes: ***, **, and * indicates statistically significant levels of 1%, 5% and 10%

In line with expectations of the first hypothesis which predicts a positive relationship between leverage ratio and the asset growth, the coefficient of the explanatory variable is found to be positive and significant with a coefficient .96 and $p<0.01$, respectively. One percent increase (decrease) in asset growth leads to a 0.96 percent increase (decrease) in the growth rate of Leverage 1 ratio. Consequently, the null hypothesis is rejected for H1; thus, the independent variables have significant explanatory power on bank leverage. The positive coefficient of asset growth makes it clear that the ratio of banks leverage is procyclical between the years 2005–2014. Banks increase their Leverage 1 ratio in the years that their total asset enlarges and they decrease their Leverage 1 ratio when their total asset narrows. In literature, Adrian and Shin (2010), Çalışkan (2011), Kalemli-Özcan, Sorensen and Yeşiltaş (2011) and Binici and Köksal (2012) prove the procyclicality of Leverage 1 ratio.

A positive and significant relation was found between size, CPI and leverage 1 ratio. It is determined that other things being equal, bigger (smaller) banks have higher (lower) Leverage 1 ratios. This is related to the concept of "too-big-to-fail", which claims that bigger banks need additional capital, leverage and liquidity requirements (Labonte, 2015). Consistent with the study of Çalışkan (2011), a positive relationship is found between CPI and Leverage 1 ratio. One percent increase in the rate of inflation reduces the growth rate of leverage by 0.007 percent. However, the result of this relation is not as strong as Çalışkan's study because of the different time periods included in each study.

The second model has a goodness of fit measure that defined by adjusted R square, 0.51 percent. The Hausman test result with a chi-square value 0.2755 led us to choose random effect panel data analysis for this model. Consistent with the expectations, a positive and strong relation is found to be statistically valid. The results state that one percent increase in asset growth will lead to an increase by 1.31 percent in leverage ratio. The results of the panel data analysis with respect to the control variables show the significance of asset size and CPI as to their relationship with leverage. Similar to Leverage 1 ratio, Leverage 2 ratio is affected by asset size and inflation positively too. The coefficient of the asset size is found to be positive and significant with a coefficient .0034 and significance level at 10 percent. The other control variable inflation is significantly associated with the dependent variable Leverage 2 ratio between 2005 and 2014 with a coefficient value of .0001082 and significance level at 1 percent, respectively. Consequently, the positive and significant coefficient of Leverage 2 ratio which is the ratio of total debt to total equity demonstrate again that the Turkish banks' leverage is procyclical between the years 2005–2014.

The positive and significant influence of asset growth on Leverage 3 indicate that Turkish bank's leverage, calculated by dividing the ratio of the sum of the total debt and off-balance sheet liabilities to total equity, is also procyclical. The coefficient of the asset growth is .95 and the significance level is 1%. The relationship between Leverage 3 ratio and asset size and inflation is found to be insignificant during the period 2005–2014.

Motivated by the study of Binici and Köksal (2012), the effect of asset growth on Leverage 4 and 5 ratios is researched in the four and fifth model. The results related to the interaction between leverage ratios and asset growth report a negative and significant influence with a coefficient -.67 and -.69 in years 2005 and 2014, respectively, which support the argument presented by Binici and Köksal. However, the association between leverage ratios and control variables is found to be statistically insignificant.

Asset growth is significantly associated with the dependent variable Leverage 6 which is the ratio of Tier 1 capital to adjusted assets. Fixed effect panel data analysis is used based on the Hausman test result that has a chi-square value of 0.0475. The significance level is 1% with a coefficient value -.83. Consistent with the expectations, a negative relation is obtained between asset growths and Leverage 6 ratios during the period 2005–2014. Additionally, similar to Leverage 1 ratio and Leverage 2 ratio, the results relating to the control variable size and inflation turned out to be significant for the observation period with significance level $p<0.01$ and $p<0.05$. There is a negative relationship between asset size and Leverage 6. This interaction is positive for inflation with a coefficient of .0003.

An increase in asset growth gives rise to an increase in the leverage ratio that is calculated by deducting the ratio of total equity to total asset from one. The positive and significant coefficient of the dependent variable Leverage 7 is demonstrated by .35 and $p<0.01$. This finding is in line with the expectations revealed in previous empirical studies by Gropp and Heider (2009 and Kalemli-Ozcan, Sorensen and Yesiltas (2011). The control variable size and CPI, which is employed in the model to control the impact of differences and external factors, is found to be insignificant.

The results of the analysis with respect to the dependent variable Leverage 8 is consistent with the prediction that the ratio of the value-at-risk to total equity has a positive interaction with asset growth with a significance level of 1% and a coefficient value of 1.92. The positive and significant influences of asset growth on Leverage 8 indicate that leverage eight is also procyclical. Contradiction as to the findings of the explanatory variable, the relation between control variables size and CPI and Leverage 8 ratio is found to be statistically insignificant.

After determining the procyclical behavior of the Turkish banking sector, we add participant and development and investment bank as dummy variables to see whether and how the results change. D1 represents participant banks and D2 represents development and investment banks. Table 4.8 below shows the outcomes of our second analysis.

Table 4.8: The Relationship between Leverage and Asset Growth Considering Banking Groups

	Leverage-1	Leverage-2	Leverage-3	Leverage-4	Leverage-5	Leverage-6	Leverage-7	Leverage-8
Asset Growth	.977 ***	1.334***	.960***	-.700***	-.842***	-.833***	.351 ***	1.826***
	(.052)	(.067)	(.217)	(.141)	(.154)	(.049)	(.024)	(.543)
Size	.059***	.069***	.068	-.018	-.021	-.059***	.009	.184
	(.018)	(.023)	(.075)	(.049)	(.053)	(.017)	(.008)	(.188)
CPI	.000**	.000**	-.000	.000	.000	.000**	-.000	.001
	(.000)	(.000)	(.000)	(.000)	(.000)	(.000)	(.000)	(.001)
D1	.072***	.083***	.087	-.012	-.016	-.074***	.010	.285
	(.025)	(.0323)	(.105)	(.068)	(.074)	(.023)	(.012)	(.262)
D2	.086***	.103***	.101	-.028	-.034	-.086***	.015	.261
	(.026)	(.033)	(.108)	(.070)	(.077)	(.024)	(.012)	(.271)
Constant	-.307***	-.364***	-.326	.090	.109	.304***	-.055	-.892
	(.085)	(.109)	(.352)	(.228)	(.249)	(.079)	(.039)	(.881)
N	360	360	360	360	360	360	360	360
R-squared	0.513	0.541	0.056	0.067	0.079	0.474	0.387	0.034

(Leverage-1: Total Assets / Total Equity, Leverage-2: Total Debt / Total Equity, Leverage-3: (Total Debt +Off Balance Sheet Liabilities) / Total Equity, Leverage-4: (Tier 1 Capital-Regulatory Deductions) / (Total Assets +Off Balance Sheet Liabilities), Leverage-5: (Tier 1 Capital-Regulatory Deductions) / (Total Debt + Off Balance Sheet Liabilities), Leverage-6: Tier 1 Capital / Adjusted Assets, Leverage-7: 1- (Total Equity / Total Assets), Leverage-8: VaR / Total Equity)

Notes: ***, **, and * indicates statistically significant levels of 1%, 5% and 10%

The results indicate that the leverage of the participation banks and development and investment banks is procyclical. There is a statistically significant relationship between Leverage 1 (total Assets over total equity), Leverage 2 (total debt over total equity), Leverage 6 (tier 1 capital / adjusted assets) and asset growth for participant and development and investment banks.

4.2 Determinants of leverage

4.2.1 Data and sample selection

The data used in this part of the book also covers the period between January 2005 and December 2014. The databases of BDDK and Central Bank of Turkey are used for the identifying the dependent and independent variables of the models. The sample comprises only banking sector information during the ten years (one hundred and twenty months) observation period. Leverage 1 ratio, which is the ratio of total assets to total equity, is selected as a dependent variable.

4.2.2 The variables

This subsection provides a detailed explanation of the variables included in the model that were applied in the second part of the book. The dependent, explanatory and control variables are summarized in Table 4.9 with their abbreviations and definitions.

4.2.2.1 Size

The size of asset has been used by the utilization of numerous proxies in previous studies. Various versions of calculations have been done for measuring size. In some studies, the natural logarithm of assets has been used as a proxy for size (Padron et al., 2005). Average value of total assets (Chung, 1993), total assets at book value (Scott and Martin, 1975), and the market value of the firm (Graham, 2000) are the other size proxies that have been used in financial literature. For determining the nonfinancial firm asset size, the mostly used proxy is the natural logarithm of net sales (Titman and Wessels, 1988; Rajan and Zingales, 1995; Wiwattanakantang, 1999; Graham, 2000; Ozkan, 2004; Gaud et al., 2005). If a firm is large, that is to say, has more tangible assets and lower market-to-book ratio, which is obtained by dividing the value of the firm's stock to the book value of its assets; then, it is expected that this firm's leverage has a tendency to be higher. These proxies clearly demonstrate that firms take financial distress risk into consideration while determining their capital structure. Large firms are less affected by financial distress since they have more diversified sources of cash to face an unexpected cash shortfall. They have more tangible assets, including machines and inventories, which could be exchanged for money more easily, and they have low market-to-book ratio that stands for new growth opportunities such as future investment activities (Berlin, 2011). The other discussion is that informational asymmetries are less important for larger firms compared to smaller firms because all things about larger firms are brought into the public eye more constantly than smaller firms. According to Fama and Jensen (1983), large firms need to disclose more information to the public, they should be more transparent than smaller firms, and they have to reduce information asymmetry costs to provide suitable conditions for equity financing. Large firms can diversify their investment projects in a broader base and limit the financial distress risk in a particular line. So, the risk of financial distress is a smaller threat to large companies. Additionally, in his study, Chen (2004) explains that large firms are attractive to the equity market due to their reputation and this situation makes it easier for them to get out of financial distress.

There are different points of view about the direction of the effect of size on leverage. According to Trade-Off Theory, the size of asset and leverage are positively related to each other. Several reasons for this positive relationship are given in literature. For example, in their study, Graham, Lemmon and Schallheim (1998) state that large companies have more stable or not often changeable cash flows because of being more diversified and they have the opportunity to use the advantage of the economies of scale in issuing securities (Graham et al., 1998). They may have more good conditions than smaller firms in entering easily into the credit markets and can borrow under better circumstances (Ferri and Jones, 1979; Wiwattanakantang, 1999).

In opposition to the view of trade-off model, some of the studies proved a negative relation between size and leverage. In their studies, Marsh (1982), Titman and Wessels (1988), Rajan and Zingales (1995), Kremp et al. (1999) and Chen (2004 determine a negative relationship between leverage and size. Rajan and Zingales (1995) find a negative relation between size and leverage for German firms. Although the liquidation process is very costly for small firms and they are more careful about avoiding potential danger of financial distress, large firms have less debt than small firms in Germany. They suggest that the reason for this negative relationship arises from information asymmetries, which give more opportunity to the large firms for issuing informationally sensitive securities rather than issuing debt (Rajan and Zingales, 1995). In their study, Kremp et al. (1999) also provide some proof related with the findings of Rajan and Zingales (1995) and argue that the characteristics of the German bankruptcy law and banking system that provide better protection to creditors than the other countries cause this negative relationship in Germany rather than asymmetrical information. Marsh (1982) examines how companies in the UK make their choice through equity and debt between 1959 and 1974, and finds that market conditions and the past history of security prices play a big role in choosing between debt and equity. He states that small firms are more suitable to be indebted than large firms because of having difficulties to enter the equity capital market and tend to depend seriously on bank loans for their funding requirements. Chung (1993) assumes that large firms have smaller agency cost associated with the asset substitution and under-investment problems and this may cause differentiation between the long- and short-term borrowing for firms of different size. The findings of the study indicate that those large firms have lower long-term debt ratio and higher short-term debt ratio than small firms.

In addition to all these studies, there are some studies that could not find any correlation between firm size and leverage ratio (Remmers, Stonehill, Wright and Beekhuisen 1975, Ferri and Jones, 1979; Kim and Sorensen, 1986; Toy et al., 1974 and; Ozkan, 2004). Motivated by the study of Toy et al. (1974), neither growth rate of assets nor earnings risk are very helpful indicators for predicting debt ratio differences across countries or even within countries. In their study, Ferri and Jones employ four different proxies to measure size for determining this relationship. Total sales, total assets at book value, the average level of total assets over the current asset and the average level of sales over the same time interval are used by Ferri and Jones, and no straightforward relation is obtained. In literature, Ozkan (2001) conducted one of the studies for empirically testing UK firms' capital structure determinants with panel data analysis, using natural logarithm of sales as a size proxy. According to test results, he could not find a significant relation between size and leverage.

In this study, we use the natural logarithm of asset as a proxy for the size of banks which is in line with most empirical studies. We are expecting a positive relationship between Turkish banks size and leverage.

4.2.2.2 Collateral

Following the definition used mostly in empirical literature, collateral is calculated by dividing the total of securities, treasury bills, bonds, cash and due from banks to total assets (Binici and Köksal, 2012). There is no general agreement for the direction of the relationship between collateral and leverage. Trade-Off Theory and Agency Theory assume that there is a positive relationship between collateral and leverage based on the reducing effect of tangible asset on financial distress. The study of Rajan and Zingales (1995), Titman and Wessels (1988), Caprio and Demirguç Kunt (1998) and Frank and Goyal (2009) support a positive relation. On the other hand, there are also works supporting the opposite. DeAngelo and Masulis (1980), Correa, Basso and Nakamura (2007), Booth et al. (2001) and Gropp and Heider (2009 find a negative relationship between collateral and leverage. In their study, Octavia and Brown (2010) couldn't find any statistically significant relationship. Since there are different opinions, no prediction is made for the impact of collateral on the Turkish banks' capital structure decision.

4.2.2.3 Profit

Firms' profitability is considered to be one of the factors that affect firms' financial leverage. Thus, there are a lot of studies regarding the determination of the influence of firm indebtedness by the firms' profitability level. Operating income over sales, operating income over total assets (Titman and Wessels, 1988), the return on assets (Wiwattanakantang, 1999), total of pre-tax profit and interest expense over total assets (Rajan and Zingales, 1995; Ooi, 1999; Ozkan, 2004; Gaud et al., 2005) could be named as the profitability measures that are utilized to capture the impact of the association between leverage and profitability which have been used in literature.

There are different assumptions about the effect of profitability on leverage. The Trade-Off Theory claims that the profitable firms will use more debt because of having a high tax burden and low bankruptcy risk, so there is a positive relationship between profitability and leverage (Sayılgan et al., 2006). On the other hand, the Pecking Order Theory predicts a negative relationship between these two important variables on the ground that profitability is a success indicator and the successful companies do not need to be indebted heavily to the external world. They choose to provide their funding with internal sources which are gathered from their past profits rather than providing their financing needs with external sources. It is indicated that observed capital structure of firms will be a sign of the cumulative requirement for external financing. As also emphasized in the study of Myers and Majluf (1984), profitable firms with slow growth rate would choose retained earnings rather than external sources as their main source of financing and unprofitable firms which run in the same sector would choose external financing to fund their operations. Therefore, unprofitable firms will have higher leverage ratios compared to the profitable firms.

However, there are some studies which have found a positive relation between these variables, there are also strong empirical proofs on the negative association between profitability and leverage. Donaldson (1961), Allen (1991), Rajan and Zingales (1995), Wiwattanakantang (1999), Chen (2003) and Gaud et al. (2005) support the Pecking Order Theory and conclude in their studies that the firms with large profits use retained earnings, while firms with small profits use more external funds to finance their operations since their internal funds are not sufficient. Rajan and Zingales (1995) document a significant and negative relationship between leverage and profitability and conclude that if large firms issue less equity then smaller firms, then the negative influence of profitability on leverage should strengthen as firm size get bigger (Rajan and Zingales, 1995). There are also some studies that cannot be precisely pinpointed as to how these variables interact.. For example, Ooi (1999) conducted a study to determine the capital structure of UK firms and could not find any significant effect of profitability on leverage. In another similar study, by searching UK firms, Ozkan (2001) discovers that profitability has a negative impact on the borrowing decisions but past profitability has a positive impact on debt ratio.

In this study, we used total of pre-tax profit and interest expense over total assets as a proxy for profitability following Rajan and Zingales (1995), Ooi (1999), Ozkan (2001), Gaud et al. (2005). In line with the above-provided reasoning, we are expecting a negative relationship between profitability and leverage.

4.2.2.4 Inflation

From the firm perspective, the theories of capital structure state that size, profit, collateral, liquidity and some other firm-specific variables are key attributes that determine the capital structure. In addition to the company-specific attributes as discussed by various researchers, the macroeconomic factors such as economic growth rate, inflation rate, capital market development, government policy, etc., also have an influence on the capital structure decision of companies. Inflation is one of the macroeconomic factors and indicates the extent to which the price of goods and services of an economy increases over a certain period of time. It is a measure of the depreciation of the currency of a country. In an economy, if the prices of goods and services rise, the purchasing power of money is reduced. Inflation is an imbalance between the expansion of money supply and economic growth. If the amount of money grows faster than the economy, this usually leads to high inflation rates. Inflation can also be caused by an imbalance between supply and demand. If there is a high demand for scarce products, their prices rise and this leads to inflation. There are a number of ways to measure the inflation of an economy. The consumer price index (CPI) is one of the most commonly used methods of inflation measurement, taking into account the price changes of a standard commodity basket. A too fast-growing economy can have high rates of inflation and a depreciation of the currency with the consequent reduction in purchasing power. An economy with low inflation or even deflation, on the other hand, maybe stagnating. It is the task of the central bank to find a balance by monitoring inflation and adjusting interest rates accordingly. The purchasing power parity compares the purchasing power of two different countries. This can be both within a single currency area and between different currency areas. This is the case when two identical goods can be purchased at the same value in both locations. The starting point is that a certain monetary unit must have the same purchasing power in every country in the world. This also means that a similar product would have to be sold at the same price all over the world. Otherwise, different transactions would be possible which called as arbitrage transactions. From this, it can be deduced that the exchange rate fluctuations between two currencies serve to compensate price differences. Because purchasing power can differ widely in different economies, a simple measurement of GDP at current exchange rates is not sufficient for comparability; it would represent a GDP measure distorted by exchange rate fluctuations.

The absolute purchasing power parity (PPP) is similar to the law of one price. The concept of the uniform price law means that the prices of the same products should be the same in different countries when measured in a single currency. The absolute PPP indicates that the exchange rate of the ratio of the two countries must take into account the price level. However, this is not easy. In reality, there are market imperfections such as non-transferable inputs, transport costs, duties, quotas and so on. The relative PPP, therefore, takes account of these shortcomings in the market and relaxes the relationship between the exchange rate and the price levels of two countries. It does this by taking into account the relationship between the changes in the exchange rate and the changes in the ratio of price levels.

Booth, Aivazian, Demirguç-Kunt and Maksimovic (2001) state that higher real economic growth make book-debt ratios move in a positive direction, and higher inflation makes it move in a negative direction. That's why they suggest that companies can borrow against real, but not inflationary growth possibility. Although the inflation which expresses the monetary value of the business assets upward, higher interest rates and the monetary risk based on inflation lead a decline in debt ratios. But it is a little different when they use market-based leverage. They couldn't find any significant relation between market-based debt ratio and inflation. In another study, Beck, Demirguç-Kunt and Maksimovic (2008) point out that the increase in inflation rate does not have any significant impact on the overall function of debt financing, but is connected with an increased use of leasing and development finance.

There are some studies which suggest a positive relation between inflation and leverage. Taggart (1985) state that the real value of tax deductions on debt is higher if there is an expectation that inflation will be high. In this manner, the Trade-Off Theory expresses an outcome in advance that leverage is positively related with the expected inflation. On the other hand, Market Timing Theory also develops a positive relation between expected inflation and leverage when executives spend debts and the expected inflation is highly relative to current interest rates (Frank and Goyal, 2009).

4.2.2.5 Gross domestic product

Gross domestic product (GDP) is a measure of the economic performance of a country for a given period. It measures the value of domestic goods and services. It is taken as an indicator of the size and health of an economy. The gross domestic product provides information about the production of domestic goods and services after deduction of intermediate consumption and imports. A distinction according to the calculation method exists in the nominal and real GDP. The calculation of the nominal gross domestic product is based on current market prices and there is an influence of inflation and deflation on the level of GDP. In order to eliminate this impact, the real GDP is calculated with the prices of a base year (with constant prices).

The literature shows the importance of macroeconomic factors in the determination of banks' capital structure decisions. The GDP growth rate is one of these macroeconomic variables that the relationship direction of it is not accurately described. Even literature presents alternative results of the relation between GDP and leverage, the Pecking Order Theory estimates a positive relation between leverage and GDP since economic growth is related with the growth of the company and promotes new investment opportunities and financing needs. In their study, Ozkan (2001) and Gropp and Heider (2007) use real GDP as a proxy for economic growth and find a positive relation between leverage and GDP growth based on the reason that during the good times, the firm used debt financing to finance their expansion programs. On the other hand, the Trade-Off Theory estimates a negative relation between GDP and leverage on account of causing higher loss of value during financial distress, when there is a scarcity of firms' tangible assets relative to available investment opportunities in a high growth environment (Köksal and Orman, 2015 pp. 13–14). Korajezyk and Levy (2003 and Demirguç-Kunt and Maksimovic (1996) demonstrate a negative relation between leverage and macroeconomic growth.

4.2.2.6 Money supply

Money is the umbrella term for several key indicators used by the central bank to measure the money circulating in the national economy. The money in circulation is divided into classes that are based on availability. Quickly available money is assigned into group M1. All cash and money which can be withdrawn daily from accounts are included in M1. The monetary amounts M2 and M3, on the other hand, include long-term money. M2 contains M1 plus deposits with an agreed maturity of up to two years (term deposits) as well as deposits with an agreed term of notice of up to three months (savings deposits).

It is important to keep the growth of the money under control. If the amount of money is too large, the rate of inflation may rise so much that it will harm the economy. If too little money is in circulation, this can affect economic growth. Financial policymakers must carefully balance growth and inflation and pursue either a restrictive or a loose monetary policy. In the case of restrictive monetary policy, the central bank is trying to reduce the amount of money. In the case of a loose monetary policy, on the other hand, the amount of money circulating is increased.

The Pecking Order Theory states that during economic growth companies evidence greater profit and use internal financing as earnings. To avoid a high inflation rate, aggregate demand is increased with the growth of credit and the quantity of money supplied. In the opposite case, during economic downturns with a low-interest rate, bank credits also begin to decline and consequently there will be a decline in corporate capital structure (Mokhova and Zinecker 2014, p. 532). Ozkan (2004) and Ariff, Taufiq and Shamsher (2008) find a negative relation between money supply and leverage for non- financial firms. They suggest that the reason is the high amount of money in circulation boost the liquidity in the market and ultimately reduce the effective interest rates.

4.2.2.7 Exchange rate

The exchange rate is the price for the unit of a currency expressed in units of foreign currency. Companies that are borrowing in terms of foreign currency will be affected by fluctuations in exchange rates, as they will repay their debts in foreign currency. Therefore, firms must take into account the influence of currency risk and other factors related with currency risk while making a choice about the use of foreign debt. Particularly, firms almost certainly make a risk-return tradeoff between the advantage of lower foreign borrowing cost and a possible rise in financial risk through exchange rate uncertainty. Because there are two types of debt, internal and external debt, the theory of optimal capital structure, accounts for both of these debts. But, it is necessary to broaden these theories by adding debt type factors. (Allayannis, Brown and Klapper, 2002, pp. 2–3). Ozkan (2001) find a positive relation between nominal exchange rate and leverage.

4.2.2.8 Number of banks

As a bank-specific variable, a number of banks express the total amount of commercial, participation and development and investment banks. Since there is a positive relationship between the number of banks and bank size, it is estimated that there is a positive relation between the number of banks and leverage.

After finding that Turkish bank's leverage is procyclical, we tried to figure out which bank-specific and macroeconomic variables affect leverage. Size, collateral, profit and number of banks are chosen as bank-specific variables. On the other hand, inflation, GDP growth, money supply and exchange rate are selected as macroeconomic explanatory variables. Table 4.9 below provides the list of the dependent and explanatory variables together with their abbreviations and definitions.

Table 4.9: Variable, Abbreviations and Definitions

Variable	Abbreviation	Definition
Leverage	leverage1	the ratio of total assets to total equity
Size	size	natural logarithm of total assets
Collateral	collateral	total of securities, treasury bills, bonds, cash and due from banks to total assets
Profit	profit	total of pre-tax profit and interest expense over total assets
Inflation	cpi	the rate of consumer price index inflation
GDP Growth	Gdp	annual percentage change of gross domestic product
M-2 Growth	m2	money supply
Exchange Rate	Exchange	real effective exchange rate
Number of Banks	banknumber	total number of banks

4.2.3 Descriptive statistics

Summaries about the measures are provided in Table 4.10 for describing the basic feature of the variables. It contains the descriptive statistics of all variables included in the empirical part of the second study for the ten-year period between 2005 and 2014, inclusive. Based on the findings provided in Table 4.10 below, the mean of size is 5.9194 with a standard deviation of 0.22. The average ratio of the total of securities, treasury bills, bonds, cash and due from banks to total assets is 27,55, and it has a small standard deviation of 4,18. Additionally, the wide range of distribution is not too big. On the other hand, profit has a mean value of 4,4 with a standard deviation of 2,5. An evaluation of the minimum and maximum values of

.0041839 and .1078257 reveal the wide range of distribution belonging to the variable profit expressing that a considerable amount of variability exists in terms of the total of pre-tax profit and interest expense over total assets. As a macroeconomic variable, inflation that represents the rate of consumer price index inflation has a mean value of 174.4782. The standard deviation is very high with a ratio of 39.31. That means there is diversity in terms of inflation ratios between 2005 and 2014.

Table 4.10: Descriptive Statistics of Variables

	Mean	Std. Dev.	Min.	Max.
leverage1	7.916	.564	6.378	9.189
size	5.920	.228	5.490	6.299
collateral	.276	.042	.203	.347
profit	.044	.025	.004	.108
cpi	174.478	39.313	114.490	248.820
gdp	4.296	4.146	-4.826	9.157
m2	.015	.017	-.042	.094
exchange rate	111.826	7.274	95.860	127.730
number of banks	49.442	1.413	47	53

The mean value of GDP growth which is measured as the annual percentage change of gross domestic product is 4.2960, and it ranges from -4.1461 to 9.1569 in the period of analysis. For the money supply, descriptive statistics show an average value of 1.51 with a standard deviation of 1.75. It ranges from -4.24 to 9.43. Unlike the money supply, the exchange rate has a high standard deviation. The mean value of exchange rate is 111.826 and it ranges between 95.86 and 127.73. The average value of total number of banks is 49.44, and deviation from this value is very little. The total number of banks in Turkey varies between 47 and 53 during the period of 2005 to 2014.

Table 4.11 demonstrates the Pearson correlation coefficients between explanatory variables utilized in the analysis. According to results displayed below, it can be stated that the model utilized is not corrupt by the problem of multicollinearity.

Table 4.11: Correlation Matrix

	leverage1	size	collateral	profit	cpi	gdp	m2	exchange	banknumber
leverage1	1								
size	0.544	1							
collateral	-0.466	-0.822	1						
profit	-0.013	-0.307	0.201	1					
cpi	0.516	0.991	-0.838	-0.327	1				
gdp	-0.239	-0.188	0.463	-0.072	-0.174	1			
m2	-0.123	-0.108	0.061	-0.080	-0.106	0.081	1		
exchange	-0.611	-0.479	0.456	0.268	-0.493	0.113	0.015	1	
banknumber	-0.532	-0.865	0.646	0.247	-0.814	0.269	0.220	0.336	1

4.2.4 Empirical research model

Cross section regression analysis deals with data about different variables during the same time periods. The main assumption of cross-sectional data is random sampling, where at a certain time, units are chosen as randomly from the population (Wooldridge, 2002).

In their study, Gujarati and Porter (2004) define cross section as "*Cross-section data are data on one or more variables collected at the same point in time*". Furthermore, they touch on one of the most important problems of cross section which is heterogeneity.

Our statistical model is constructed as in Equation 11 below:

$$Leveragei = \beta 0 + \beta 1 sizei + \beta 2 collaterali + \beta 3 profiti + \beta 4 cpii + \beta gdpi + \beta 5 m2i + \beta 6 exchangei + \beta 7 banknumberi + \varepsilon i \qquad \textbf{(Eq. 11)}$$

where:

size is natural logarithm of total assets; *collateral* is the total of securities, treasury bills, bonds, cash and due from banks to total assets; *profit* is total of pre-tax profit and interest expense over total assets; *cpi* is the rate of consumer price index inflation; *gdp* is annual percentage change of gross domestic product; *m2* is money supply; *exchange* is real effective exchange rate; and *banknumber* is the total number of banks. The variable ε is the error term that includes unobserved factors that affect leverage.

Null hypothesis says that the change in independent variables does not have any effect on leverage ratio and alternative hypothesis states that independent variables have a significant influence on leverage.

H_0: The independent variables do not explain bank leverage ($\beta i = 0$)
H_1: The independent variables explain bank leverage ($\beta i \neq 0$)

4.2.5 Data analysis and results

A key research subject of modern corporate finance is the choice of the optimal capital structure of companies. The main matter is whether and how financing decisions affect the cost of capital and the market value of a company. The choice of the optimal capital structure also has immense importance for financial management. The starting point is the question of whether the capital costs are reduced for a given capital volume by a change in the level of debt or an exchange of the financing instruments on the liabilities side, thereby increasing the market value of the company. The different theories of the capital structure reflect the relationship between different bank-specific variables and the financing structure. They try to explain how the debt ratio is correlated with bank-unique data such as company size, asset structure, growth potential, profitability, liquidity and to what degree the debt ratio is affected from macroeconomic variables such as GDP, interest rate and inflation. In order to limit the trend in the explanatory variables, a trend term has been added into the model.

Table 4.12 contains the predicted effects of explanatory variables of this study, size, collateral, profit, inflation, gross domestic product, money supply and exchange rate and a number of banks on leverage according to Modigliani-Miller, Agency, Trade-Off and Pecking Order Capital Structure Theories. Also, the behavior of leverage is different for companies and banks. Therefore, the forecasted effects of financial and non- financial firms and bank-firm specific and macroeconomic variables on leverage are included.

Table 4.12: Predicted Effects of Explanatory Variables on Leverage

Variable	Studies on firms	Studies on banks	M&M Theorem	Agency Theory	Trade-off Theory	Pecking Order Theory
size	+/-	+		+	+	-
collateral	+/-	-/not significant		+	+	
profit	-	-	+		+	-
cpi	+	+				+
gdp	+/-	+/-/not significant			-	+
m2						
exchange						
banknumber	+	+		+	+	

Table 4.13 shows the signs and the levels of significance of the explanatory variables' coefficients. The results of the analysis are consistent with the prediction that leverage has an interaction with size, profit, inflation, gross domestic product, exchange rate and the number of banks. The positive influence of size on leverage with a significance level of 1% and a coefficient value of 29.63217 indicates that leverage increases with the size of the asset. That means when a firm has more tangible assets and when its market-to-book ratio, which is obtained by dividing the value of the firm's stock to the book value of its assets, is lower, it is expected that this firm's leverage has a tendency to be higher. In the same direction as the studies in the literature, we couldn't find any significant relation between collateral and leverage. However, in contrast to the literature we find a positive relation between profitability and leverage. The Trade-Off Theory claims that the profitable firms will use more debt because of having a high tax burden and low bankruptcy risk, so there is a positive relationship between profitability and leverage (Sayılgan, Karabacak and Küçükkocaoğlu, 2006). On the other hand, on the ground that profitability is a success indicator and the successful companies do not need to be indebted heavily to the external world, the Pecking Order Theory predicts a negative relationship between these two important variables.

Table 4.13: The Relationship between Leverage and Bank-Specific and Macroeconomic Variables

	Asset/Equity
Size	29.632***
	(1.671)
Collateral	1.406
	(.999)
Profit	2.650***
	(.769)
Cpi	.054***
	(.006)
Gdp	-.013**
	(.006)
m2	-.916
	(1.102)
Exchange	-.015***
	(.003)
Banknumber	.111***
	(.037)
Trend	.243***
	(.013)
Constant	-195.897***
	(12.008)
Observations	120
R-squared	0.887

Notes: ***, **, and * indicates statistically significant levels of 1%, 5% and 10%.

Parallel to the bank-specific explanatory variables, macroeconomic variables also have a statistically significant effect on leverage. The results show that leverage is positively and significantly affected by the consumer price index, which is consistent with previous empirical work. This means that any increase in prices of goods and services causes higher leverage ratios. The variables GDP and exchange rate have negative and significant effects on banks leverage. Although the literature presents alternative results of the relation between GDP and leverage, the Pecking Order Theory estimates a positive relation between leverage and GDP since economic growth is related with the growth of the company and promotes new investment opportunities and financing needs. In their study, Ozkan (2001) and Gropp and Heider (2007) use real GDP as a proxy for economic growth and find a positive relation between leverage and GDP growth based on the reason that during the good times, firms use debt financing to finance their expansion programs. On the other hand, the Trade-Off Theory estimates a negative relation between GDP and leverage, on account of causing higher loss of value during financial distress when there is not enough tangible assets relative to existing investment opportunities in an advanced environment (Köksal and Orman, 2014, pp. 13–14). Additionally, the number of banking institutions operating in Turkey during the period 2005–2014 has a significant effect on the leverage ratio. As the number of banks increases, the leverage ratio increases.

5 Conclusion

This section provides a general review of the study and a summary of the research findings. The main aim of this study is determining the leverage behavior of Turkish banking sector. The study also focuses on the relationship between leverage and bank-specific and macroeconomic variables. Supporting the previous studies, evidence is provided for the positive relation between asset growth and leverage, and it is shown that during boom phase banks use more debt in comparison to the recession. Another remarkable finding is that there is a strong relation between Turkish banking leverage ratio and size, profit, number of banks, inflation, gross domestic product and exchange rate.

Recent crises highlighted once again the importance of banks in the economy. Once again it became clear that banks are moving in the same direction with the economy. This procyclical behavior of banks attracted the attention of policymakers, accounting and finance professionals, and academicians and has become a controversial topic. In addition, many opinions have been raised about the causes of procyclicality. Some of the policymakers and academicians blame the accounting standards, some of them the banking regulations and others the credit rating agencies for causing procyclicality. For example, fair value accounting is found guilty because of the recognition of assets at fair value. That means that the fluctuations in the economy can then be recognized in the value of assets. This leads to the fact that, in the case of banks, they are getting higher and higher profits from the fair value valuation in times of economic booms. On the other hand, during financial recession, the downside of the market valuation quickly became apparent. The assets that were highly valued in the past begin to be depreciated again due to falling market values. As a result, the crisis begins to feed the crisis. Another accused regulation is Basel II accord. It is known that Basel I had several deficiencies. It was not risk sensitive enough and it did not adequately meet the challenges of banks' risk management. These deficiencies recognized by the authorities and corrected within the framework of Basel II. In this respect, Basel II was already a significant step towards a more stable financial system. Nevertheless, the crisis has also shown the weaknesses of Basel II. One of the weaknesses of Basel II is the fact that it does not correctly identify certain risks. It focuses on individual institutions and did not cover systemic risks. However, the crisis has shown that the nature and extent of systemic risks in the financial sector are not only linked to the potential illiquidity or the insolvency of large financial institutions, but also to the tight interweaving of financial institutions, markets and infrastructures.

Except fair value accounting and Basel accords, the amount of debt used to finance a firm's assets which are called as leverage also cause procyclicality. In phases with low-interest rate and high rate of return, it is attractive for financial institutions to raise their return by increasing their borrowing. This causes an increase in the creditworthiness and recovers the economy. These procyclical effects also play an important role in the economic downturn when there is a simultaneous decline in the value of the assets and a much more cautious lending. Low asset prices can lead to a smaller leverage, and as a result of the leverage effect, banks are forced to repurchase assets on a large scale, which is only possible with considerable losses in the event of a poor market situation.

In this study, it is shown that Turkish banks' leverage moves in the same direction with economic conditions. The data used in the empirical part of the book covers the period between January 2005 and December 2014, inclusive. The sample comprises all the commercial, participation and development-investment banks information during the ten-year, one hundred and twenty months, observation period. Different leverage definitions have been used to prove that this is not a coincidence. Some of these leverage definitions are known by everyone and are very common in the literature. On the other hand, some definitions are not very much popular. Such as total assets to total equity and total debt to total equity ratios are the most commonly used leverage definitions and they show exactly what percentage of the bank's assets are financed by debt. Conversely, some of the researchers argue that standard calculations of leverage are not suitable for financial institutions as they do not take both debt and non-debt liabilities of banks into consideration. That's why in this study we also use one minus the ratio of equity over assets as a leverage ratio that describes the decomposition of leverage. Using these eight different definitions of the leverage ratio, it is shown that procyclicality is a natural part of the real and financial sectors of the Turkish economy. The implication is that the financial institutions change their activities in response to the changing economic environment. This behavior may create a vicious circle and expand the cyclical fluctuations of the real economy and produce a negative feedback to the financial sector itself. Therefore, to eliminate this negative feedback, there should be a countercyclical leverage ratio interval.

The determinants of the bank capital structure, which are tried to be found by different researchers in different ways, also constitute a part of this book. The studies on capital structures have become an important subject matter in corporate finance with the study of Modigliani and Miller (1963). Their remarks deal with the influence of a company's degree of indebtedness on its capital costs and market value. They assume a complete capital market in equilibrium and under this assumption, they state that capital structure decisions have no effect on the market value of a company. This means that the proportion of a company's equity and borrowed capital is irrelevant to the asset position of the company. Based on this basic theory, many theories have been developed later and along with these new theories, the missing aspects of the old theories have been completed. In spite of the fact that a great number of studies in literature have analyzed the impact of bank and macroeconomic characteristics on capital structure, unfortunately, there is limited evidence for Turkey.

In this study, the determinants of bank capital structure for Turkish banks were investigated by using different bank-specific and macroeconomic variables. It is examined whether size, collateral, profit, number of banks, inflation, GDP growth, M-2 growth and exchange rate have an impact on the bank's capital structure. It is important to find the determinants of bank capital structure to make appropriate capital structure decisions that is suitable for banks' financing needs. Regarding the macroeconomic factor, the results provide evidence for a positive relation between leverage and inflation and a negative relation between leverage and gross domestic product and exchange rate. On the other hand, findings regarding the relationship between bank-specific factors demonstrate the significant and positive influence of size, profit and number of banks on the proxy of bank capital structure.

This book helps to clarify the cyclical behavior of banks leverage. Related with literature, this study provides recent evidence from Turkey with respect to the link between the leverage and asset growth. The study puts forward new attempts for consideration. In order to provide further research, this book can be expanded by a larger panel data set or by increasing number of alternative leverage ratios and control variables which will further increase the reliability of the study. Additionally, even though this study provides evidence for the existence of a significant relation between some bank-specific and some macroeconomic variables, future research can be advanced by increasing the number of explanatory variables. Also, the determinants of bank capital structure can also be examined for crisis and normal periods to see whether there is any change.

References

Books

Balthazar, L. (2006). *From Basel 1 to Basel 3: The Integration of State-of-the-Art Risk Modeling in Banking Regulation*. Palgrave Macmillan.

Berk, J. and DeMarzo, P. (2011). *Corporate Finance*, 2nd edition. Pearson Education Limited.

Bessler, W., Drobetz, W. and Kazemieh, R. (2011). "Factors Affecting Capital Structure Decisions," *Capital Structure and Corporate Financing Decisions: Theory, Evidence, and Practice*. John Wiley & Sons, Inc.

Copeland, T.E. and Weston, J.F. (1988). *Financial Theory and Corporate Policy*. Addison-Wesley Publishing Company.

Craig R.S., Davis E.P. and Pascual A.G. (2006). "Sources of Procyclicality in East Asian Financial Systems," in Gerlach S. and Gruenwald P. (eds), *Procyclicality of Financial Systems in Asia*, pp. 55–123, Palgrave Macmillan.

Donaldson, G. (1961). *Corporate Debt Capacity: A Study of Corporate Debt Policy and the Determination of Corporate Debt Capacity*. Division of Research, Graduate School of Business Administration, Harvard University.

Gujarati, D.N. and Porter, D.C. (2004). *Basic Econometrics*, 4th edition. The McGraw–Hill Companies.

Ronald, W.M., Merle, T.W. and Edgar, A.N. (1996). *Finance: Introduction to Institutions, Investments, and Management*. South-Western Publication.

Ross, S., Westerfield, R. and Jaffe, J. (2013). *Corporate Finance*, 10th edition. McGraw–Hill Education.

Taggart, R.A. (1985). "Secular Patterns in the Financing of U.S. Corporations," in Benjamin M. Friedman, (ed), *Corporate Capital Structures in the United States*. University of Chicago Press, pp. 13–80.

Van Horne, J.C. and Wachowicz, J.M. (2008). *Fundamentals of Financial Management*, 13th edition, Pearson Education Limited.

Wooldridge, J.M. (2002). *Econometric Analysis of Cross Section and Panel Data*. The MIT Press, Cambridge, Massachusetts.

Articles

Adrian, T. and Shin, H.S. (2010). "The Changing Nature of Financial Intermediation and the Financial Crisis of 2007–09." Federal Reserve Bank of New York Staff Reports, No. 439.

Allayannis, G., Brown, G. and L. Klapper, (2002). "Capital Structure and Financial Risk: Evidence from Foreign Debt Use in East Asia." *Journal of Finance*, Vol. 58, No. 6, pp. 2667–2709.

Allen, D.E. (1991). "The Determinants of the Capital Structure of Listed Australian Companies: The Financial Manager's Perspective." *Australian Journal of Management*, Vol. 16, No. 2, pp. 103–125.

Allen, L. and Saunders, A. (2004). "Incorporating Systemic Influences into Risk Measurements: A Survey of the Literature." *Journal of Financial Services Research (2004)*, Vol. 26, pp. 161–191.

Altman, E.I. and Kao, D.L. (1992). "Rating Drift of High Yield Bonds." *Journal of Fixed Income*, March, pp. 15–20.

Amato, J.D. and Furfine, C.H. (2003). "Are Credit Ratings Procyclical?" BIS Working Papers No. 129.

Ang J., Chua J. and McConnell, J. (1982). "The Administrative Costs of Corporate Bankruptcy: A Note." *The Journal of Finance*, Vol. 37, No. 1, pp. 219–226.

Ariff, M., Taufiq, H. and Shamsher, M. (2008). "How Capital Structure Adjusts Dynamically during Financial Crises." Bond Business School Publications.

Athanasoglou, P.P. and Daniilidis, I. (2011). "Procyclicality in the Banking Industry: Causes, Consequences and Response." Bank of Greece, manuscript in Greek.

Athanasoglou, P.P., Daniilidis, I. and Delis, M. (2013). "Bank Procyclicality and Output: Issues and Policies." *Journal of Economics and Business*, Vol. 72, pp. 58–83.

Baglioni, A., Beccalli, E., Boitani, A. and Monticini, A. (2012). "Is the Leverage of European Banks Procyclical?" *Empirical Economics*, Vol. 45, No. 3, pp. 1251–1266.

Bangia, A., Diebold, F. and Schuermann, T. (2000). "Ratings Migration and the Business Cycle, With Applications to Credit Portfolio Stress Testing." Financial Institutions Center Working Paper, Vol. 00–26.

Barth, M.E. (1994). "Fair Value Accounting: Evidence from Investment Securities and the Market Valuation of Banks." *The Accounting Review*, Vol. 69, No. 1, pp. 1–25.

Barth, M.E. Landsman, W.R. and Wahlen, J.M. (1995). "Fair Value Accounting: Effects on Banks' Earnings Volatility, Regulatory Capital, and Value of Contractual Cash Flows." *Journal of Banking and Finance*, Vol. 19, No. 3–4, pp. 577–605.

Baxter, N.D. (1967). "Leverage, Risk of Ruin and the Cost of Capital." *The Journal of Finance*, Vol. 22, No. 3, pp. 395–403.

Bayrakdaroğlu, A., Ege, İ. and Yazıcı, N. (2013). "A Panel Data Analysis of Capital Structure Determinants: Empirical Results from Turkish Capital Market." *International Journal of Economics and Finance*, Vol. 5, No. 4, pp. 131–140.

Beccalli, E., Boitani, A. and Giuliantonio, S. (2015). "Leverage Pro-cyclicality and Securitization in US Banking." *Journal of Financial Intermediation*, Vol. 24, No. 2, pp. 200–230.

Beck, T., Demirguc-Kunt, A. and Maksimovic, V. (2008). "Financing Patterns Around the World: Are Small Firms Different?" *Journal of Financial Economics*, Vol. 89, No. 3, pp. 467–487.

Behn, M., Haselmann, R. and Wachtel, P. (2016). "Procyclical Capital Regulation and Lending." *Journal of Finance*, Vol. 71, No. 2, pp. 919–956.

Berlin, M. (2011). "Can We Explain Banks' Capital Structures?" *Business Review*, No. Q2, pp. 1–11.

Bevan, A. and Danbolt. J. (2004). "Testing for Inconsistencies in the Estimation of UK Capital Structure Determinants." *Applied Financial Economics*, Vol. 14, pp. 55–66.

Binici, M. and Köksal, B. (2012). "Is the Leverage of Turkish Banks Procyclical?" *Central Bank Review*, Vol. 12, pp. 11–24.

Booth, L., Aivazian, V., Demirguc-Kunt, A. and Maksimovic, V. (2001). "Capital Structures in Developing Countries." *The Journal of Finance*, Vol. 56, No. 1, pp. 87–130.

Borio C., Furfine C. and Lowe P. (2001). "Procyclicality of the Financial System and Financial Stability: Issues and Policy Options." BIS Papers, No. 1.

Borio, C. and Zhu, H. (2008). "Capital Regulation, Risk-Taking and Monetary Policy: A Missing Link in the Transmission Mechanism?" BIS Working Papers, No. 268.

Breuer, P. (2000). "Measuring Off-Balance-Sheet Leverage." IMF Working Paper, WP/00/202.

Brunnermeier, M.K. (2009). "Deciphering the Liquidity and Credit Crunch 2007–2008." *Journal of Economic Perspective*, Vol. 23, No. 1, pp. 77–100.

Caprio, G.J. and Demirguc-Kunt, A. (1998). "The Role of Long-Term Finance: Theory and Evidence." World Bank Research Observer, World Bank Group, Vol. 13, No. 2, pp. 171–189.

Cesaroni, T. (2015). "Procyclicality of Credit Rating Systems: How to Manage It." Money and Finance Research Group. Working Paper no: 109.

Chen, J.J. (2004). "Determinants of Capital Structure of Chinese-Listed Companies." *Journal of Business Research*, Vol. 57, pp. 1341–1351.

Chen, J. and Strange, R. (2005). "The Determinants of Capital Structure: Evidence from Chinese Listed Companies." *Economic Change and Restructuring*, Vol. 38, No. 1, pp. 11–35.

Chittenden, F., Hall, G. and Hutchinson, P. (1996). "Small Firm Growth, Access to Capital Markets and Financial Structure: Review of Issues and an Empirical Investigation." *Small Business Economics*, Vol. 8, No. 1, pp. 59–67.

Chung, K.H. (1993). "Asset Characteristics and Corporate Debt Policy: An Empirical Test." *Journal of Business Finance and Accounting*, Vol. 20, No. 1, pp. 83–98.

Claessens, S., Ghosh, S.R. and Mihet, R. (2014). "Macro-Prudential Policies to Mitigate Financial System Vulnerabilities." IMF Working Paper WP/14/155.

Correa, C.A., Basso, L.F.C. and Nakamura, W.T. (2007). "What Determines the Capital Structure of the Largest Brazilian Firms? An Empirical Analysis Using Panel Data." *Journal of International Finance and Economics*.

Covas, F. and Fujita, S. (2010). "Procyclicality of Capital Requirements in a General Equilibrium Model of Liquidity Dependence." *International Journal of Central Banking*. December 2010 issue, pp. 137–173.

Cuadra, G., Sanchez, J.M. and Sapriza, H. (2009). "Fiscal Policy and Default Risk in Emerging Markets." The Federal Reserve Bank of Richmond Working Paper, No: 09–01.

Çalışkan, A. (2011). "Leverage Behavior of Turkish Banks: How Did They Escape The Global Crisis?" *İktisat İşletme ve Finans*, Vol. 26, No. 307, pp. 75–104.

DeAngelo, H. and Masulis, R. (1980). "Optimal Capital Structure under Corporate and Personal taxation." *Journal of Financial Economics*, Vol. 8, No. 1, pp. 3–29.

Deesomsak, R., Paudyal, K. and Pescetto, G. (2004). "The Determinants of Capital Structure: Evidence from the Asia Pacific Region." *Journal of Multinational Financial Management*, Vol. 14, pp. 387–405.

Demirguc-Kunt, A. and Maksimovic, V. (1996). "Stock Market Development and Financing Choices of Firms." *Word Bank Economic Review*, Vol. 10, pp. 341–369.

Demirguc-Kunt, A. and Detragiache, E. (1998). "The Determinants of Banking Crises in Developing and Developed Countries." *IMF Staff Papers*, Vol. 45, No. 1, pp. 81–109.

D'Hulster, K. (2009). "The Leverage Ratio: A New Binding Limit on Banks." Crisis Response Note, No. 11. World Bank.

Eisenhardt, K.M. (1989). "Agency Theory: An Assessment and Review." *The Academy of Management Review*, Vol. 14, No. 1, pp. 57–74.

Fama, E.F. and French, K.R. (2002). "Capital Structure Choices." *Critical Finance Review*, Vol. 1, pp. 59–101.

Fama, E.F., Fisher, L., Jensen, M.C. and Roll, R. (1969). "The Adjustment of Stock Prices to New Information." *International Economic Review*, Vol. 10, No. 1, pp. 1–21.

Fama, E.F. and Jensen. M.C. (1983). "Separation of Ownership and Control." *Journal of Law and Economics*, Vol. 26, pp. 301–325.

Fattouh, B., Harris, L. and Scaramozzino, P. (2008). "Non-Linearity in the Determinants of Capital Structure: Evidence from UK Firms." *Empirical Economics*, Vol. 34, No. 3, pp. 417–438.

Ferri, M.G. and Jones, W.H. (1979). "Determinants of Financial Structure: A New Methodological Approach." *The Journal of Finance*, Vol. 34, No. 3, pp. 631–644.

Financial Accounting Series Statement of Financial Accounting Standards. (2006). "Fair Value Measurements." No. 157.

Flannery, M.J. and Rangan, K.P. (2006). "Partial Adjustment toward Target Capital Structures." *Journal of Financial Economics*, Vol. 79, pp. 469–506.

Frank, M.Z. and Goyal, V.K. (2009). "Capital Structure Decisions: Which Factors are Reliably Important?" *Financial Management*, Vol. 38, pp. 1–37.

Gambera, M. (2000). "Simple Forecasts of Bank Loan Quality in the Business Cycle." Emerging Issues Series. Supervision and Regulation Department, Federal Reserve Bank of Chicago.

Gaud, P., Jani, E., Hoesli, M. and Bender, A. (2005). "The Capital Structure of Swiss Companies: An Empirical Analysis Using Dynamic Panel Data." *European Financial Management*, Vol. 11, No. 1, pp. 51–69.

Geanakoplos, J. (2010). "The Leverage Cycle." University of Chicago Press NBER Macroeconomics Annual 2009, Vol. 24, p. 1–65.

Giordana, G. and Schumacher, I. (2012). "The Impact of the Basel III Liquidity Regulation on the Bank Lending Channel: A Luxemburg Case Study." Cahier de Etude, Working Paper no. 61. Banque Centrale Du Luxemburg.

Graham J.R. (2000). "How Big are the Tax Benefits of Debt?" *The Journal of Finance*, Vol. 55, No. 5, pp. 1901–1942.

Graham, J.R., Lemmon M. and Schallheim J. (1998). "Debt, Leases, Taxes, and the Endogeneity of Corporate Tax Status." *Journal of Finance*, Vol. 53, No. 1, pp. 131–162.

Grigore, M.Z. and Ştefan-Duicu, V.M. (2013). "Agency Theory and Optimal Capital Structure." *International Conference: CKS – Challenges of the Knowledge Society*, May 2013, p. 862–868.

Gropp, R. and Heider, F. (2009). "The Determinants of Bank Capital Structure." European Central Bank, Working Paper Series, No. 1096.

Guttentag, J.M. and Herring R.J. (1986). "Disaster Myopia in International Banking." Essays in International Finance, No. 164.

Hahn, F. (2002). "The Effects of Bank Capital on Bank Credit Creation. Panel Evidence from Austria." WIFO Working Paper 188.

Hardouvelis, G.A. (2010). "Actions for a Less Procyclical Financial System." *Economy & Markets*, Eurobank Research, Vol. 5, No. 5.

Harris, M. and Raviv, A. (1991). "The Theory of Capital Structure." *The Journal of Finance*, Vol. 46, No. 1, pp. 297–355.

Haugen, R.A. and Senbet, L.W. (1978). "The Insignificance of Bankruptcy Costs to the Theory of Optimal Capital Structure." *The Journal of Finance*, Vol. 33, No. 2, pp. 383–393.

Heshmati, A. (2001). "The Dynamics of Capital Structure: Evidence from Swedish Micro and Small Firms." *Research in Banking and Finance*, Vol. 2, pp. 199–241.

Hovakimian, A., Hovakimian, G. and Tehranian, H. (2004). "Determinants of Target Capital Structure: The Case of Dual Debt and Equity Issues." *Journal of Financial Economics*, Vol. 71, pp. 517–540.

Hovakimian, A., Opler, T. and Titman, S. (2001). "The Debt-Equity Choice." *Journal of Financial and Quantitative Analysis*, Vol. 36, No. 01, pp. 1–24.

Hsiao, C. (2006). "Panel Data Analysis—Advantages and Challenges." Wise Working Paper Series, WISEWP0602.

Huang, S. and Song, F.M. (2006). "The Determinants of Capital Structure: Evidence from China." *China Economic Review*, Vol. 17, pp. 14–35.

Özkan, S. (2004). "Post Keynesyen Finansal Kırılganlık Yaklaşımının Türkiye'de Finansal Krizlere (1990–2001) Uygulanması." *İktisat/işletme ve Finans*, Vol. 218, pp. 51–77.

Jensen, M.C. and Meckling, W.H. (1976). "Theory of the Firm: Managerial Behavior, Agency Costs and Ownership Structure." *Journal of Financial Economics*, Vol. 3, No. 4, pp. 305–360.

Jensen, M.C. (1986). "Agency Costs of Free Cash Flow, Corporate Finance, and Takeovers." *The American Economic Review*, Vol. 76, No. 2, pp. 323–329.

Jouida, S. and Hallara, S. (2015). "Capital Structure and Regulatory Capital of French Banks." *Procedia Economics and Finance*, Vol. 26, pp. 892–902.

Kalemli Ozcan, S., Sorensen, B. and Yesiltas, S. (2011). "Leverage across Firms, Banks, and Countries." *Journal of International Economics*, Vol. 88, No. 2, pp. 284–298.

Kaminsky, G.L., Reinhart, C.M. and Vegh, C.A. (2004). "When It Rains, It Pours: Procyclical Capital Flows and Macroeconomic Policies." *NBER Macroeconomics Annual 2004*, Vol. 19, pp. 11–53.

Khalid, S. (2011). "Financial Reforms and Dynamics of Capital Structure Choice: A Case of Publically Listed Firms of Pakistan." *Journal of Management Research*, Vol. 3, pp. 1–16.

Kim, E.H. (1978). "A Mean-Variance Theory of Optimal Capital Structure and Corporate Debt Capacity." *The Journal of Finance*, Vol. 33, No. 1, pp. 45–63.

Kim, W. and Sorensen, E. (1986). "Evidence on the Impact of the Agency Costs of Debt on Corporate Debt Policy." *Journal of Financial and Quantitative Analysis*, Vol. 21, No. 4, pp. 131–144.

Kim, M.K. and Wu, C. (1988). "Effects of Inflation on Capital Structure." *The Financial Review: The Official Publication of the Eastern Finance Association*, Vol. 23, No. 2, p. 183.

Korajczyk, R. and Levy, A. (2003). "Capital Structure Choice: Macroeconomic Conditions and Financial Constraints." *Journal of Financial Economics*, Vol. 68, No. 1, pp. 75–109.

Kraus, A. and Litzenberger, R.H. (1973). "A State-Preference Model of Optimal Financial Leverage." *The Journal of Finance*, Vol. 28, No. 4, pp. 911–922.

Kremp, E., Stöss E. and Gerdesmeier. D. (1999). "Estimation of a Debt Function: Evidence from French and German Firm Panel Data", in Sauvé A., Scheuer M. (eds), *Corporate Finance in Germany and France.*, Deutsche Bundes bank/Banque de France.

Laux, C. and Rauter, T. (2016). "Procyclicality of U.S. Bank Leverage." *Journal of Accounting Research, Vol. 55, No. 2, pp. 237–273.*

Leland, H. and Pyle, D. (1977). "Informational Asymmetries, Financial Structure, and Financial Intermediation." *Journal of Finance*, Vol. 32, No. 2, pp. 371–87.

Lowe, P. and Stevens, G. (2004). "Procyclical Financial Behavior: What can be done?" in Gerlach S. and Gruenwald P. (eds), "Procyclicality of Financial Systems in Asia", Palgrave Macmillan.

Marinsek, D., Pahor, M., Mramor, D. and Lustrik, R. (2015). "Do European Firms Behave as if they Converge toward a Target Capital Structure?"

Journal of International Financial Management and Accounting, Vol. 27, No. 2, pp. 97–125.

Marsh, P. (1982). "The Choice between Equity and Debt: An Empirical Study." *Journal of Finance*, Vol. 37, No. 1, pp. 121–144.

Mazur, K. (2007). "The Determinants of Capital Structure Choice: Evidence from Polish Companies." *International Advances in Economic Research*, Vol. 13, pp. 495–514.

Modigliani, F. and Miller, M.H. (1958). "The Cost of Capital, Corporation Finance and the Theory of Investment." *The American Economic Review*, Vol. 48, No. 3, pp. 261–297.

Modigliani, F. and Miller, M.H. (1963). "Corporate Income Taxes and the Cost of Capital: A Correction." *The American Economic Review*, Vol. 53, No. 3, pp. 433–443.

Mokhova, N. and Zinecker, M. (2014). "Macroeconomic Factors and Corporate Capital Structure." *Procedia – Social and Behavioral Sciences*, Vol. 110, pp. 530–540.

Myers, S.C. (1984). "The Capital Structure Puzzle." *The Journal of Finance*, Vol. 39, No. 3, pp. 574–592.

Myers, S.C. and Majluf, N. (1984). "Corporate Financing and Investment Decisions when Firms have Information that Investors do not have", *Journal of Financial Economics*, Vol. 13, pp. 187–221.

Myers, S.C. (2001). "Capital Structure." *The Journal of Economic Perspectives*, Vol. 15, No. 2, pp. 81–102.

Nijathaworn, B. (2009). "Rethinking Procyclicality – What Is It Now and What Can be Done?" BIS review 160/2009.

Novoa, A., Scarlata, J. and Sole, J. (2009). "Procyclicality and Fair Value Accounting." IMF Working Paper, Vol. 09, No. 39.

Octavia, M. and Brown, R. (2010). "Determinants of Bank Capital Structure in Developing Countries: Regulatory Capital Requirement versus the Standard Determinants of Capital Structure." *Journal of Emerging Markets*, Vol. 15, No. 1, pp. 50–62.

Ooi, J. (1999). "The Determinants of Capital Structure – Evidence on UK Property Companies." *Journal of Property Investment & Finance*, Vol. 17, No. 5, pp. 464–480.

Orman, C. and Köksal, B. (2015). "Structure of Debt Maturity across Firm Types Working Papers 1521, Research and Monetary Policy Department, Central Bank of the Republic of Turkey.

Ozkan, A. (2001). "Determinants of Capital Structure and Adjustment to Long Run Target: Evidence from UK Company Panel Data." *Journal of Business Finance and Accounting*, Vol. 28, pp. 175–198.

Padron, Y.G., Apolinario, R.M.C., Santana, O.M., Conception, M., Martel, V. and Sales, L.J. (2005). "Determinant Factors of Leverage: An Empirical Analysis of Spanish Corporations." *Journal of Risk Finance*, Vol. 6, No. 1, pp. 60–68.

Pettengill, G.N. and Lander, D.M. (2015). "Response of the Cost of Equity to Leverage: An Alternative Perspective." *Journal of Business Strategies*, Fall 2015, Vol. 32, No. 2, pp. 110–138.

Psillaki, M. and Daskalakis, N. (2009). "Are the Determinants of Capital Structure Country or Firm Specific?" *Small Business Economics*, Vol. 33, No. 3, pp. 319–333.

Rajan, R.G. (1994). "Why Bank Credit Policies Fluctuate: A Theory and Some Evidence." *The Quarterly Journal of Economics*, Vol. 109, No. 2, pp. 399–441.

Rajan, R.G. (2005). "Has Financial Development Made the World Riskier?" NBER Working Paper, No. 11728.

Rajan R.G. and Zingales L. (1995). "What Do We Know About Capital Structure? Some Evidence from International Data." *Journal of Finance*, Vol. 50, No. 5, pp. 1421–1460.

Remmers, L., Stonehill, A., Wright, R. and Beekhuisen, T. (1975). "Industry and Size as Debt Ratio Determinants in Manufacturing Internationally." *Financial Management*, Vol. 3, No. 2, pp. 24–32.

Ryan, S.G. (2008). "Fair Value Accounting: Understanding the Issues Raised by the Credit Crunch." Council of Institutional Investors.

Salas, V. and Saurina J. (2002). "Credit Risk in Two Institutional Settings: Spanish Commercial and Saving Banks." *Journal of Financial Services Research*, Vol. 22, No. 3, 203–224.

Sayılgan, G., Karabacak, H. and Küçükkocaoğlu, G. (2006). "The Firm-Specific Determinants of Corporate Capital Structure: Evidence from Turkish Panel Data." *Investment Management and Financial Innovations*, Vol. 3, No. 3, pp. 125–139.

Scott, J.H. (1976). "A Theory of Optimal Capital Structure." *Bell Journal of Economics*, Vol. 7, No. 1, pp. 33–54.

Scott D. and Martin, J. (1975). "Industry Influence on Financial Structure." *Financial Management*, Vol. 4, pp. 67–73.

Sharpe, I. (1995). "Determinants of Capital Structure of Australian Trading Banks." *Asia Pacific Journal of Management*, Vol. 12, No. 2, pp. 97–121.

Shyam-Sunder, L. and Myers, S.C. (1999). "Testing Static Tradeoff against Pecking Order Models of Capital Structure." *Journal of Financial Economics*, Vol. 51, pp. 219–244.

Titman, S. and Wessels, R. (1988). "The Determinants of Capital Structure Choice." *The Journal of Finance*, Vol. 43, No. 1, pp. 1–19.

Toy, N., Stonehill, A., Remmers, L., Wright, R. and Beekhuisen, T. (1974). "A Comparative International Study of Growth, Profitability and Risk as Determinants of Corporate Debt Ratios in the Manufacturing Sector." *Journal of Financial and Quantitative Analysis*, Vol. 9, No. 5, pp. 875–86.

Vo, X.V. (2017). "Determinants of capital structure in emerging markets: Evidence from Vietnam." *Research in International Business and Finance*, Vol. 40, pp. 105–113.

Warner, J.B. (1977). "Bankruptcy Costs: Some Evidence." *The Journal of Finance*, Vol. 32, No. 2, pp. 337–347.

Wiwattanakantang Y. (1999). "An Empirical Study on the Determinants of the Capital Structure of Thai Firms." *Pacific-Basin Finance Journal*, Vol. 7, pp. 371–403.

Zadeh, A.A., Barth, M.E. and Landsman, W.R. (2017). "The Contribution of Bank Regulation and Fair Value Accounting to Procyclical Leverage." *Review of Accounting Studies*, Forthcoming. Available at SSRN: https://ssrn.com/abstract=2300497.

Other Publication

Bank of International Settlements 79th Annual Report (2009).

Bank for International Settlements 84th Annual Report. (2014).

Basel III: The Liquidity Coverage Ratio and Liquidity Risk Monitoring Tools. (2013).

Broden, D. and Olovsson, K. (2011). "Fair Value Accounting and Procyclical Behavior in the Swedish Banking Sector." University of Gothenburg School of Business, Economics and Law Master's Thesis.

European Central Bank Monthly Bulletin, January 2005.

European Central Bank Financial Stability Review. (2009).

Fair Value Measurements. (2005). PwC Report.

Federal Reserve Bulletin. (2003). Vol. 89, No: 9. September 2003.

Financial System Review. (June 2009). Bank of Canada.

Labonte, M. (2015). "Monetary Policy and the Federal Reserve: Current Policy and Conditions." CRS Report.

Landau, J.P. (2009). "Procyclicality – What It Means and What Could Be Done." Remarks by Mr Jean-Pierre Landau, Deputy Governor of the Bank of France, at the Bank of Spain's Conference on Procyclicality and the Role of Financial Regulation, Madrid, May 4, 2009.

Monthly Bulletin January. (2005). European Central Bank.

Nguyen, H. and Kayani, Z. (2013). "Determinants of Banks' Capital Structure in Asia: A Comparison amongst Developed and Developing Countries." Lunds Universitet, School of Economics and Management, Department of Business Administration, degree project, Master of Science in Business and Economics.

Papagianni, E.F. (2013). "The Determinants of Bank Capital Structure." International Hellenic University, master thesis.

Park, H.M. (2011). "Practical Guides to Panel Data Modeling: A Step by Step Analysis Using Stata." International University of Japan, Public Management & Policy Analysis Program.

Report of the President's Working Group on Financial Markets. (1999).

Reyna, T.O. (2007). "Panel Data Analysis Fixed and Random Effects using Stata." http://dss.princeton.edu/training/.

Standard & Poor's Corporate Rating Criteria. (2002).

Sha'ban, M., Girardone, C. and Sarkisyan, A. (2016). "The Determinants of Bank Capital Structure: A European Study." https://www.city.ac.uk/__data/assets/pdf_file/0007/336373/SHABAN,-Mais-.pdf.

www.ingramcontent.com/pod-product-compliance
Ingram Content Group UK Ltd.
Pitfield, Milton Keynes, MK11 3LW, UK
UKHW020152290926
15471UKWH00005B/828

9 783631 746219